CHARTER STORM

STORM

WAVES OF CHANGE SWEEPING OVER PUBLIC EDUCATION

MARY SEARCY BIXBY
TOM R. DAVIS

GREENLEAF
BOOK GROUP PRESS

Published by Greenleaf Book Group Press
Austin, Texas
www.gbgpress.com

Distributed by Greenleaf Book Group

For ordering information or special discounts for bulk purchases, please contact Greenleaf Book Group at PO Box 91869, Austin, TX 78709, 512.891.6100.

Publisher's Cataloging-in-Publication data is available.

Paperback ISBN: 978-1-62634-581-2
Hardcover ISBN: 978-1-62634-588-1
eBook ISBN: 978-1-62634-582-9

Part of the Tree Neutral® program, which offsets the number of trees consumed in the production and printing of this book by taking proactive steps, such as planting trees in direct proportion to the number of trees used: www.treeneutral.com

TreeNeutral

Printed in the United States of America on acid-free paper

18 19 20 21 22 23   10 9 8 7 6 5 4 3 2 1

First Edition

*This work is dedicated to educational thought changers
who have borne the challenge of pushback
and have still forged ahead, putting students first.*

*It is our wish that our thinking will inspire
a continued effort to move with assertive and passionate grit.*

TABLE OF CONTENTS

FOREWORD

ONE MIGHT THINK the ominously titled *Charter Storm: Waves of Change Sweeping over Public Education* predicts the demise of the chartered schools as an education reform strategy. Far from it: In *Charter Storm*, veteran educators Mary Bixby and Tom Davis offer a realpolitik summary of the history and current state of chartered schools, combined with clear and unambiguous analysis and advice for practitioners, opponents, and observers.

Bixby and Davis draw from their extensive personal experience as leaders within both the traditional public and chartered systems. Davis is a veteran public school educator with decades of experience in teaching and leading traditional public schools at both the school site and central office levels. More recently, Davis has served as a consultant and executive coach for innovative education organizations, including chartered schools.

Bixby is a twenty-five-year veteran of California's chartered schools, having founded The Charter School of San Diego in 1994, which later grew into the Altus family of schools. Currently, Altus successfully serves thousands of students in Southern California across multiple districts and counties. With substantial experience working in parochial, traditional public, and chartered schools, Bixby is a keen observer of the sector and has earned and received every award and accolade that a charter school leader can garner in California. Both Bixby and Davis can see the chartered sector through multiple lenses and perspectives as few others can.

More than twenty-five years of helping draft charter school laws in dozens of states and at the federal level has taught this observer that chartered schools are primarily a creature of state law. Key features of state charter school laws vary widely, so cross-state comparisons and analyses are fraught with difficulty. While their expertise is primarily based in California, Bixby and Davis are unique among observers in that they extensively researched both the California and national chartered school scene, comparing their home-state experiences and observations with similarly situated experts across the country. They somehow managed to gain access to a who's who of chartered school thinkers and leaders in every major charter state, interviewing many repeatedly over a lengthy and thorough research effort.

During the mid- and late 1990s, I had the opportunity to work on and help draft many of the charter school laws in states and localities visited by the authors. It has been fascinating for me to compare notes with Bixby and Davis throughout their past several years of research and drafting. They are among a tiny number of individuals who have built a deep understanding of chartering—both in California and nationally—and they are the only practitioners to have done so. Bixby and Davis's deep experience base allowed them to see the forest through the trees, boiling down often fraught details to key economic, political, and strategic themes.

Charter Storm traces key elements in the development of the chartered schools concept, from the "originals" who developed the concept and nurtured it to its rapid growth in more recent years. Bixby relates these to her firsthand experiences as one of California's earliest, most innovative, and most successful chartered school founders. While steadily growing her network of schools for more than twenty-five years, Bixby has been a leader among chartered school leaders in her San Diego–area home base and at a statewide level.

This has given her a deep, firsthand understanding of how school districts, policy makers, the media, and others view and respond to chartered schools. An entire chapter in this book focuses on the many myths that opponents and others have developed to characterize charter schools, including why they persist.

Bixby and Davis offer a tough-love analysis. The burden of dispelling myths, they argue, rests on chartered reform proponents themselves. It's up to them, not the media or researchers, to "shed light on the shining example[s]" within the chartered schools sector.

Charter Storm places chartering in the larger education reform landscape, categorizing chartered schools among the "Big R" reform efforts, distinguishing it from "Little R" efforts that often appear larger than they are. Chartering is a Big R reform because it fundamentally challenges the sustainability and survival of the traditional public school system. While this Big R status is what gives the chartered schools sector its punch, it's also what generates resistance and potentially crippling backlash. "Wherever chartered schools are growing, pushback is occurring," write Bixby and Davis, who use familiar analogies (e.g., David and Goliath) to illustrate the complex political and economic challenges facing the charter sector. Novices will appreciate this clear explanation and unpretentious analysis, while veteran observers will sharpen their understanding through references and analogies to cutting-edge thinkers, including Malcolm Gladwell and Malcolm Baldrige (Bixby's experience leading a Baldrige Award–winning organization shows here).

The pushback against chartered schools, in turn, "threatens the very strength of the original design of chartered schools: to experiment and develop new ways to operate and inspire students to reach their greatest potential." The first of two chapters on pushback defines the term in the context of tipping points, offering an insightful explanation of several factors that influence school districts' individual tipping points. This chapter then explains how these common factors can lead to various forms of pushback from stakeholders and vested interests—largely without regard to the vagaries of state law or local context.

A second chapter on pushback offers concrete examples, challenging both chartered school and traditional public school advocates to question their assumptions. For chartered advocates, it illustrates how hot-button charter issues (such as colocating charter schools on traditional public school campuses, varying approaches to charter authorizing, and funding equity) challenge chartered school proponents. It also challenges proponents of traditional public schools to do the same and offers concrete strategic suggestions for both, including how focusing on student needs and outcomes can benefit all.

The sixth chapter, titled "Observations," offers strategic analysis of various strengths, weaknesses, opportunities, and threats (SWOTs) facing the charter sector. Some of these are relatively straightforward (e.g., growing public dissatisfaction with traditional public schools), while others are less well understood (e.g., the growth of networked chartered schools and the difficulty that non-networked chartered schools face when combating pushback).

The final chapters build on the SWOT analysis and other key points, offering deeper analyses and specific suggestions to chartered school leaders, chartered school advocates, philanthropists, charter authorizers, and others.

"The jury is no longer out. The debate is moot. Chartered schools are here to stay," declare the authors in conclusion. Chartered schools will survive the many challenges facing them, but only those schools whose leaders see these challenges and adapt will do so. This optimistic conclusion must be rooted in an equally optimistic belief that chartered school leaders and others will see the challenges that Bixby and Davis identify, unify as a sector to meet the threat of pushback, and lead accordingly within their schools.

ERIC PREMACK *is the founding director of CSDC. For over twenty years, Premack has played a leading role in the development and spread of chartered schools, including helping to draft and implement chartered school policy in over twenty-five states, at the federal level, and overseas. He has developed groundbreaking chartered school policy, planning, implementation, oversight, and leadership development practices that have been emulated throughout the United States and internationally.*

ACKNOWLEDGMENTS

THERE ARE DOZENS of individuals who have contributed to this effort. Here, we recognize some of the key people who made this book possible.

Lawrence Ineno was our editor. He supported us in the development of a process for writing together. Although his professional background differs from ours, he shares with us common points of view. First, we both believe that students must be the top priority in all decision-making. Second, we hold strongly that there is a need for educational change to be allowed to flourish. Lawrence inspired us, allowed us to explore, helped us insert self-discipline into the process, and at times, mediated. A previous bestselling author on his own, he understood the role this book would play in advancing the chartered school movement and kept our feet to the fire until we fulfilled the vision for the work.

Board members and key advisors to The Charter School of San Diego and its affiliated schools called for formal documentation of what we learned. Our initial assignment was to improve our strategic planning by investigating where the future was taking chartered schools. Later, as we presented our results and understood that other people wanted to know more, they asked us to document our personal insights in the form of a book. Thanks to Eric Premack, Jed Wallace, Ted Kolderie, Senator Gary Hart, Leendert Hering, RADM (Ret.), Alfred Ferris, Jane Gawronski, Barbara Peluso, Vicki Barber, Arlene Gluck, Gregg Haggart, Jim Hernandez, Tim Morton, Joseph Watkins, Jennifer Montgomery, Roman Rubio, and David Quezada for their futuristic vision of what is possible and to deceased friends and advisors Pat Hyndman, Mark Fingerlin, David Nuffer, and John Nersesian.

Never-ending sources of support and inspiration began with our dear friend and colleague Lynne Alipio and Leadership Team members Tim Tuter, Tiffany Yandell, Jackie Robertson, Debora Giaquinta, Arline McGowan, Stephanie Starr, Wade Aschbrenner, Alissa Tuter, Rachel Thomas, and Gail Levine. In addition, we thank Alina Nuno and Angela Neri, who are among the hundreds of instructional leaders and support staff that make up the Altus Schools community.

These individuals are classic examples of all that is good in the chartered school movement. Collectively, these people and those that came before them have positively influenced over forty-four thousand student lives over the course of twenty-four years.

The interviewees played a critical role in sharing their perspectives, engaging in the highest level of honest and direct dialogue, and challenging us when they had a different view. They were the best part of the entire process. With many, we left so enthralled by their comments and the aha moments we experienced that we talked for hours and hours about what we had heard. Even today, very often we share some of the most memorable times—always with the greatest respect and appreciation.

No matter what their perspectives, we engaged a broad list of some of the most impressive professionals in the country. Whether they were senators, assembly people, superintendents, university professors, community activists, parents, students, lawyers, authors, chartered school association leaders, mayoral office staff, school principals and leaders, teachers, organizational heads of all kinds, school board members, state board and commission members, or school, district, and county leaders and staff, this endless list of people left an eternal mark on our thinking. They were interested and even curious about our findings. Our next book will center on many of them and our takeaways in terms of change-oriented leadership. Thanks to each one for sharing his or her time and energy and—most of all—for taking a chance with us.

We must recognize our families. Our spouses and our families have been the greatest support when it seemed a daunting task to even contemplate an end to the work.

Last, in our travels, we met the kindest of all people. Everywhere we went throughout the country, we experienced the United States of America at its finest. Gracious and thoughtful, everyone along the way was attentive and supportive. We were always received with respect and courtesy. When they asked, we shared that we were in the midst of an investigation to see what was happening with educational reform. They all had an opinion to share, and they all truly cared about kids and what their schooling would mean to their futures and the future of America. These people must be given an attentive ear. They know a great deal, and their expectations are worthy.

Introduction

A CHARTERED SCHOOL PRACTITIONER'S SNAPSHOT OF EDUCATIONAL REFORM

IN THE MIDST of the many dramatic events occurring around the globe, there is a not-so-silent war currently gripping the United States, and yet it is ignored by many. It centers on a critical aspect of American life—an aspect destined to affect our economy, scientific discovery, political evolution, social mores, artistic endeavors, health, crime levels, urban decline, urban development, issues of race and poverty, and overall American culture. The outcomes of today's fight will have implications for decades to come. They may even result in change that can never be reversed.

This raging war is born of a strict contrast in educational philosophies and perspectives. It affects not only every man, woman, and child currently living in the United States but also those who have not yet been born or immigrated to our shores. The battle lines are drawn in the sand.

In many ways, the powerful strength of the status quo and its decades-old structures are attempting to crush new thought and innovation.

Similar to the clash of biblical proportions between David and Goliath, the smaller, righteous challenger is circling the massive, muscle-bound image of the past, facing a brutal beating at every turn. In this analogy, Goliath personifies the public education establishment comprising school districts, school boards, administrators, teachers, and their associations. David, the small challenger, is the embodiment of a chartered school movement daring to face down an antiquated adversary bent on destruction.

Today, the educational establishment in many parts of the country is fighting for its very survival. While it is too late for some school districts, others have suddenly awakened to a radical decline in enrollments due to students attending chartered schools. For many districts that relied on their public education monopoly, there is little effort to support improvement or change. The educational establishment so casually assumed its power that it never imagined ragtag groups of innovators with a dream could seriously affect business as usual.

A Brief History of the Educational Reform Movement

Chartered schools came on the scene more than twenty years ago. Born in Minnesota and further nurtured in California, the tender movement was first greeted with a passing interest and little consideration or anticipation of where it would lead the future of public education.

The chartered school concept saw the light of day in Minnesota in 1991. When charter law was first passed, public opinion about schools in general was at low tide. Ideas relating to a new, different, change-oriented system for managing schools were churning throughout a wide variety of professional and nonprofessional individuals who cried out for educational reform. They sought a new level of flexibility and high levels of accountability.

Ted Kolderie, a brilliant thinker and visionary, succeeded in helping usher in the first bold move toward a new model for establishing public schools independent from the traditional public school monopoly that had been in place for decades.

The wild chartered school ride in California began a year later. The advent of landmark legislation passed in 1992 has undoubtedly changed the face of public education forever. Since then, the chartered school movement in California has shifted from an initial ceiling of 100 charters to more than 1,250 chartered schools today, with more than five hundred thousand students enrolled.

Early educational reformers were scruffy colonialists dumping tea into the bay. Little could anyone imagine the discontent of the masses could crystallize into a never-to-be-forgotten stand. Today, we face a battle so great on a hill so close that the sound of our challenge resonates in thousands of American neighborhoods in both urban and rural communities—nearly every place in the United States where parents have found a voice and will never again succumb to powers that do not put their children's interests first.

Through the next twenty years, chartered school momentum swept across the country, embracing a total of forty-three states (plus Washington, DC), and is undoubtedly one of the most significant changes to have moved public education in nearly fifty years. Those of us who were at the helm of change from the beginning are still in awe of what has transpired in the intervening years. Some dreamed of a national impact. Others, such as these writers, were thinking of creating a lab model that would perhaps catch fire among public education futurists and thought changers.

The Charter School of San Diego was assigned chartered school number twenty-eight by the California State Board of Education. Although deemed a start-up charter, in reality it was the spin-off of a California program known as Educational Clinic Alternatives. This alternative program aspired to stem the tide of dropouts who were sending a resounding alarm throughout the San Diego community and beyond.

The transition from a district-dependent program to a full-fledged California Public Charter School (the first of its kind in San Diego

County), while not without bumps, is a story inspiring to behold. The Charter School of San Diego came into being thanks to the dynamic efforts of a passionate and committed group of educators, businesspeople, and community supporters, an achievement all the more impressive when you realize it gave birth to one of the first charter documents, at the time only seven pages long. It was a paraphrase of state charter law and a far cry from today's extremely detailed and sophisticated applications submitted to charter authorizers.

The vision, inspiration, and support for The Charter School of San Diego originated among a group of brave, bold thinkers associated with the former San Diego Chamber of Commerce Business Roundtable for Education. As of 2018, The Charter School of San Diego has evolved into eight separate chartered schools serving 8,447 students. The schools' learning resource facilities can be found throughout Southern California. Each campus is committed to teaching students who seek an alternative setting for instruction.

Many schools have adopted the Altus model, which focuses on providing students a creative and rigorous alternative to traditional public schools. The Altus model has targeted at-risk students who are two to three years behind in English language arts and sometimes three to five years behind in math. Some students choose a self-paced and personalized educational setting. The Altus model is a student-centered and personalized approach to a school's instruction and operation. It runs on a systems-type process orientation that has delivered outstanding academic outcomes. The Altus approach to teacher development, strategic planning, accountability, and student-centered fiscal planning has earned it national recognition.

In 2015, The Charter School of San Diego was the first K–12 public school to become a National Baldrige Award recipient. US Commerce Secretary Penny Pritzker presented the award on behalf of the Office of the President of the United States. The Charter School of San Diego was awarded the honor for its demonstration of positive academic outcomes and excellence in school operation and quality. Companies that previously received this accolade include the following: Motorola Inc., Westinghouse Electric Commercial Nuclear Fuel Division, Xerox Corporation, FedEx, IBM, Ritz-Carlton (now part of Marriott International), AT&T, Texas Instruments Inc., Eastman Chemical Company, University of Wisconsin–Stout, Sharp HealthCare, Lockheed Martin Missiles, PricewaterhouseCoopers, and Boeing.

Chartered schools, along with the sudden surge in the use of technology to deliver instruction, have turned old models for instruction on their heads and created a previously unseen synergy for transformation. Change and the concept of educational reform are on the minds of everyone that pledges to be a harbinger of a futuristic movement taking students, schools, and learning communities to new heights for teaching and learning.

Charter Storm: The Rationale

Every investigation starts with a premise, a question to be answered, and a hope for how one's discoveries may unfold. Our premise was a qualitative approach to finding answers to our basic assumptions, questions, and theories. Our journey of discovery started with the following questions:

- What is the educational reform movement's current status in the United States?

- Is a desire for change dramatically disrupting public education as we know it?

We reviewed relevant data, trends, and research. During our examination, it became apparent a one-size-fits-all approach was inadequate. We noted how various regions of the country have experienced charter growth differently. The national trends we were looking for did not always present themselves in exactly the same fashion. For example, in the nation's largest cities, various schools within district boundaries evolved their particular chartered school movement.

Given the diversity of the educational reform movement, The Charter School of San Diego's board of directors charged us with making sense of these variances and addressing the question, "What decisions should we be making now to position our students, staff, and schools for a successful future?"

To discover how different regions of the country are implementing the chartered school movement, we elected to divide the United States into geographic regions. Our investigation would focus on researching and visiting each region and identifying key trends, obstacles, and successes, as well as notable outliers. We realized the importance of interviewing the professionals who play a significant role in influencing development and implementation of chartered schools.

Before we could begin our investigation, it was necessary to develop a series of assumptions. We understood some would be sustained and others would be proven false or irrelevant. From the onset, we wanted to establish our role as advocates and supporters of chartered schools.

The vast majority of our research was in medium to large metropolitan areas. We found it impossible to separate large-city chartered school policy from state policies, practices, and procedures. No city was absent of state oversight. This work represents a time interval from 2013 to 2016. As current headline news regarding educational reform demonstrates, the content remains as relevant as ever.

Our goal is to share our observations and findings. We have a definite pro–charter bias, and we have expressed our opinions throughout this book. At the same time, we took the information provided by professionals at face value. It was not our purpose to argue or discredit anyone. Our advisors strongly recommended that these findings would be helpful in both training new staff as they entered chartered schools and in further inspiring our veteran leaders to continue meeting the challenge. Our board of directors requested that we share our discoveries. This book is the result.

The Work

The most challenging aspect of writing this book was taking all the research and narrowing it down to its most salient points. We wrote hundreds of pages and distilled them within the following chapters, which comprise of the most valuable information we gathered, as well as our observations and reflections based on our cross-country investigation. We carefully charted the course for how best to allow our story to evolve. Here is a short summary of the major concepts covered in *Charter Storm*.

Chapter 1, "Market-Driven Educational Reform," examines what precipitated the design and development of the educational reform movement. It delves into the introduction of competition in the public school system that challenged the status quo, which was the long-standing monopoly vehemently protected by the establishment. This chapter touches on the history of, development of, and current efforts to slow chartered school growth, in addition to the rise of the voice of the customer.

What is the nature of this ensuing battle? Chapter 2, "David and Goliath," examines the unlikely challenge the small community of chartered schools imposed on the giant known as public education. David personifies the advocacy and passion awakened by the bold commitment of countless teachers, parents, and community members. The tragedy is that some are bent on seeing that nothing really changes, as underserved children across the nation are lost with each passing year. (Some liken the ensuing battle to Armageddon.) Goliath represents an old system, which too often is unwilling to compromise. He is fighting for his very survival. Can young David succeed and create a monumental disruption, the likes of which public education has never experienced? Can a small group of underresourced pioneers succeed in disrupting a myopic, often self-serving public education monolith?

Chapter 3, "Myths," is a straightforward guide that addresses and dispels common misconceptions surrounding chartered schools. These pose a significant threat to the educational reform movement because, if they are repeated often enough, they become today's fake news, which hurts the reputation of chartered schools.

Aside from being grossly biased, these myths become huge obstacles and thereby hamper useful and relevant change. Key factors are often ignored or minimized. Repeated efforts to mitigate a myth only seem to support the faulty base on which they are founded. The myths appear to be promulgated in areas that have a limited amount of community professional interaction or access to research.

Chapters 4 and 5, "Pushback Part 1" and "Pushback Part 2," focus on educational establishment resistance to the educational reform movement. When significant losses to district revenues occurred, the educational establishment waged a full-fledged war against chartered schools. Aggressive pushback continues today—and like a snowball setting off an avalanche, organized labor, school boards responsible for finance, and critics invested in the business of public education have initiated a major pushback.

An awareness of the tools used in pushback is essential to the survival of chartered schools. Chartered schools that are struggling to cope do not face a positive future. In fact, they probably do not face a future at all. The strong will survive. Schools with strategic plans, resources, and the political power of their communities will more than likely live to carry forth the banner of progressive change and innovation.

Chapter 6, "Observations," is a collection of our most salient observations based on our nationwide investigation. We perform a SWOT (strengths, weaknesses, opportunities, and threats) analysis of the educational reform movement.

Chapter 7, "Lessons Learned," follows up with very specific recommendations for chartered schools. We are convinced if all chartered schools create an effective plan that follows our recommendations, they will have a high chance of survival.

Chapter 8, "Philanthropy," addresses the role of benefactors in educational reform. What has attracted the big-money investors who support a radical change in how American youth are educated? This chapter explores the effect philanthropists have had on the chartered school movement and addresses common criticisms associated with philanthropy and chartered schools.

Chapter 9, "Observations on Poverty," explores poverty and public education. We examine the different approaches and perspectives that have driven public school efforts to reduce poverty, the challenges public schools face, and the role that chartered schools have played in lifting students and families out of poverty.

Chapter 10, "Authorizers," offers observations and suggestions to issues such as oversight needs. It examines the role of policy development, well-articulated policy, and the garnering of realistic projects that can help guide school districts, county offices, and states in their challenge to preserve their system.

The development of a fully collaborative approach to policy and oversight is a two-way street. Chartered schools that truly appreciate the difficulties of managing their oversight can come to a place that supports their authorizers to seek mutually agreeable solutions.

In the end, *Charter Storm* does not aspire to create a magical approach that resolves the many issues surrounding the educational reform movement of today. Instead, we see the debates occurring around the nation as a means for further exploration. This work offers many points deserving more consideration. We hope it may be used as a training manual for individuals new to the educational reform movement. We seek to inspire our veteran leaders to advance the cause for high-quality schools. Most important, we challenge all our readers to pursue reshaping an extremely adversarial landscape into a place where collaboration and recognition of mutual benefit result in educators truly placing students' needs first—and not only meeting their needs but also raising the bar on the promise of public education.

Chapter 1

MARKET-DRIVEN EDUCATIONAL REFORM

OUTSIDE THE HEATED interior of our rental car, the temperature was bitterly cold. The low, gray midday sky reminded us that we were well into a midwestern winter. Looking out from our vehicle, we witnessed block after block of empty streets. This was a ghost town built on the bones of a once-vibrant community: vacant homes where parents had previously raised their sons and daughters now plastered with Do Not Occupy signs, rusted swings and slides with No Trespassing signs where children had previously played until sunset, abandoned places of worship now for sale, and empty storefronts that signaled a once-bustling local economy.

We could see in the remnants of this community the former promise of a Norman Rockwell vision of American life. Now, however, all that remained was haunting emptiness. And for those proud Americans trying to get by that had no option but to survive in this dystopia, the absence of stores and community services made us wonder how they accessed basic resources such as food, education, and medical care.

As we slowly drove down the desolate streets, we understood why no one from the Chicago Public Schools (CPS) office offered to provide us a tour of the public schools in this area. In fact, CPS representatives advised us against visiting this part of South Chicago because of its reputation for violence. But we knew that in order to understand the impact school closures had on a community, we needed to see firsthand the neighbor-hoods where schools were being shut down and not to rely on hearsay and spotty media coverage. When we spoke with Dr. Howard Rosing, executive director of the Steans Center at DePaul University, he described how closing schools killed neighborhoods, broke the spirit of communi-ties already in despair, and was done over the objections of local leaders. He told us how South Chicago had been pushed to near revolution.

Sadly, the dismal conditions were not isolated to the Windy City. In Atlanta, St. Louis, Washington, DC, and other metropolitan areas through-out the country, we observed similar instances of local school closures wreaking havoc on communities. As a result of the neighborhood decay we witnessed, we called into question the decisions and actions taken by politi-cians and those on the front lines of public education.

Through our investigation, a broader question surfaced: Is public edu-cation in decline? According to the media, the answer is undoubtedly yes. Among those who are not sure, they often point to changes within society at large, such as the widespread deterioration of courtesy, social mores, and academic expectations from teachers and students. Even those who staunchly reject that public education is in decline acknowledge that, at least, the institution is in transition.

The question of public education's decline is most relevant to con-sumers and providers.

Consumers are not only the parents and guardians of K–12 students but also the community at large, which includes grandparents, neighbors, civic organizations that have an interest in schools, business interests such as companies that develop a workforce for the future, individuals interested in national security, faith-based organizations, and philanthropists.

Consumers also include those individuals who seek to improve the quality of life in the United States—whether they recognize it or whether they have children, they have a stake in public education.

Providers are professionals on the front line of public education and the educational establishment. The front line of public education comprises administrators, teachers, and support staff. The educational establishment includes the US Department of Education, state departments of education, county departments of education, district boards of education (including their own administrations), and associations and unions.

Troubling School Statistics

While consumers and providers may debate the causes of the problems plaguing public education as a whole, the struggles schools face today are both serious and undeniable. According to a report issued by the District of Columbia Public Schools in 2017, only 32 percent of third graders in Washington, DC, public schools can read proficiently. In 2017, Normandy School District in St. Louis County, Missouri, with a predominately African American student population, had a 73.4 percent high school graduation rate (73.2 for its black students). Clayton School District, located five miles away, has a predominately white student population and had a 98.15 percent graduation rate in 2017 (100 percent for its black students). In the 2016 fiscal year, Detroit Public Schools had a $215.9 million deficit. Overall, only 25 percent of high school graduates are proficient in math. And only 37 percent of high school graduates are proficient in reading.

Parental Expectations Dashed by a Dysfunctional System

All parents strive for the best for their children. At the top of this aspiration is securing a first-rate education. No matter urban or rural, rich or poor, according to the promise of public education, every community should offer free and equitable schools that maintain high quality and expectations.

Indeed, alongside the hope of millions of parents, the purpose of public education is to prepare young people to be responsible citizens, who intelligently exercise their right to vote, become productive individuals, and positively contribute to society—this is what we define as the educational social contract. Unfortunately, public schools as a whole have never lived up to this ideal. In fact, the gap between what public education should be and what it actually represents in communities throughout this nation continues to grow wider.

Through our investigation, we conducted interviews with mayoral offices, officials with state departments of education, state senators, assembly representatives, other civic leaders responsible for developing or influencing public education policy, representatives of the community, chartered school leaders, educational reform leaders, academics, parents, teachers, and administrators. The parents we interviewed across the country repeatedly named safety and a welcoming atmosphere as high priorities when it came to an educational setting for their children. But after visiting schools throughout the United States and interviewing consumers and providers, our research showed that most schools have consistently failed on both accounts. In *Charter Storm*, we will share our experiences in search of the answer to the following questions:

- What is the educational reform movement's current status in the United States?

- Is a desire for change dramatically disrupting public education as we know it?

Shortly after we embarked on our journey, the answers to these questions became abundantly clear. Based on our cross-country investigation and interviews, educational reform is sweeping the country in varying degrees. The desire for change is rapidly and increasingly disrupting public education as a whole.

While we found many excellent traditional public schools, in the aggregate, outstanding schools were the exception rather than the rule. This was particularly true in urban areas, where the highest concentration of our nation's children is educated and where schools consistently fall short.

What we found was a high number of schools with hostile and threatening conditions, in which rampant verbal abuse and bullying among students went largely ignored by school staff, in which teachers and administrators demonstrated powerlessness or indifference to tackling the school's biggest problems, and in which students were disengaged with the learning process.

But even in state-of-the-art, beautiful campuses located in affluent communities—far away from poverty and violence—students frequently reported feeling unsafe.

The bottom line is the systemic problems within public education are varied and extensive. Collectively, they have resulted in widespread depression and emotional withdrawal among students and a general discontent with the institution itself from students and staff alike. In the end, parents and guardians around the country are struggling to address the needs of children who are enrolled in dysfunctional schools.

Enter the Chartered School

Imagine a learning environment that maintains a student-first approach. Think about what a school would look like if teachers were equally as engaged as their students in the learning process. At its core, such a driven approach to education would engender the following four qualities:

1. **Purpose**—Students and teachers are engaged in goal-oriented work and are passionate about reaching achievable objectives.

2. **Mastery**—Students and teachers strive for excellence.

3. **Autonomy**—Students and teachers have the freedom to approach curriculum in innovative ways.

4. **Safety and Security**—Students and teachers are physically safe and secure. School sites maintain discipline and order that give teachers the ability to perform at their highest potential. Teachers are confident they are being supported by the administration.

Prior to the introduction of chartered schools, implementing such an effective and innovative framework was challenging and discouraging for those working within the existing traditional public school system, which was entrenched in bureaucracy and government regulation and constrained by the self-serving agendas of powerful special interests. Offering parents schools that upheld the preceding four qualities required a dramatic educational paradigm shift that had to work outside the public education establishment but still exist within a tax-funded structure.

This new approach would be based on a **market-driven** principle of parental choice that maintained the following premise: Each child learns differently. So rather than be bound to a one-size-fits-all model of education, where parents are limited to having their kids attend one local campus, parents could choose a school that met the particular needs of their sons and daughters. In other words, as the primary educators of their children, parents would be free to select the best instructional match for their children among a variety of schools.

In 1991, Minnesota was the first state to grant itself the power to become an **authorizer**. In public education, an authorizer is the entity given the authority to grant **charters**. Charters are written contracts that allow the creation of institutions (in this case, a new type of public school). An authorizer may be a university or a state or local organization (such as a board of education, county department of education, or an independent commission). Currently, forty-three states have charters allowing for the establishment of entities other than local school districts to offer public education.

WHAT IS MARKET-DRIVEN?

This hallmark of capitalism in the United States is an organizational characteristic and performance metric that is informed by economic forces such as supply and demand, market share, profit and loss, and competition.

Companies such as Amazon, Starbucks, and Apple have captured retail market share through their superior products and services. In a market-driven system, customers will patronize a service that welcomes them, meets or exceeds their expectations, and provides high-quality outcomes. A market-driven organization sustains itself by identifying the impact of future events and developing a plan that focuses on solvency and safeguards against future losses. Market-driven entities tend to focus on internal competencies that foster a greater responsiveness to their customers and target market.

As Ted Kolderie explained in his book *The Split Screen Strategy: Improvement + Innovation,* today, the term "charter school" refers to a type of public school. But originally, this new type of institution had no such designation. Rather, it was simply a public school created by a charter—in other words, a *chartered* public school. Chartered schools were designed to be independent institutions contracted by districts, the state, or state-designated entities. They emerged as an educational model that would usher in a breakthrough, market-driven approach to public schools.

In order to uphold the original intent of this type of public school, throughout this book, we will use the term "chartered school," rather than the more commonly used "charter school." We will also refer to non-chartered public schools as traditional public schools or traditional schools to distinguish them from chartered schools. While both chartered and traditional schools are public schools, as you will read, significant differences exist between the two.

A Brief Overview of Chartered Schools

Within educational reform, two major movements arose in the 1990s: the adoption of information technology and the legislation that created chartered schools.

Think of these two movements as "Reforms" with an uppercase *R*. Contrast these with reforms that rehashed, renamed, reshaped, and reidentified programs, projects, and concepts that already existed, were slightly modified, and then were reintroduced into the classroom or the school system. Consider these as "reforms" with a lowercase *r*. In other words, these movements have been more evolutionary than revolutionary.

The distinction between Reforms and reforms is significant because the public education establishment has pointed to little-r reforms—such as standards-based education, individualized education, and more recently, science, technology, engineering, and math (STEM) education and Common Core—to demonstrate how public education is at the forefront of continuous improvement and innovation. But little-*r* reforms such as these pale in comparison to the following Reforms.

First, the digital age dramatically changed pedagogy and school-site and district-level administration. Smart classrooms and countless online resources have transformed how educators teach and students learn. Attendance, grading, and human resources data are web-based, and technology will continue to create new possibilities for instruction and administration.

Second, from the original legislation that created chartered schools, a new market-driven option emerged that single-handedly reshaped public education.

The political and public support of chartered schools was largely in response to concerns regarding the state of public education in the early 1990s. At the time, multiple disturbing conditions called into question the health of our public education system: campus drug trafficking and gang violence; achievement gaps among the economically disadvantaged, immigrant populations, and ethnic minorities; school district budget and management scandals; teacher union malfeasance; a general lack of school accountability; and concerns over global competitiveness of our nation's youth. As a result, the future of the institution rose to the top of public discourse.

Politicians, academics, business leaders, and parents sought solutions to a system in crisis, and those passionate about educational reform went to work to determine how to solve public education's greatest problems. From these intense discussions, a market-driven approach emerged as an innovative way to combat the low standards and expectations that plagued public education.

In 1992, California enacted groundbreaking legislation that opened the doors for chartered schools. California's high profile placed a national spotlight on chartering. For the next twenty years, the chartered school movement expanded in the Golden State, as well as across the nation.

> *The introduction of a market-driven approach has become the most significant movement in public education over the past two decades.*

Those of us who were at the forefront of the chartered school movement so many decades ago look back in awe at the breathtaking progress chartered schools have made during such a short period. For example, The Charter School of San Diego (CSSD), chartered in 1993, was the twenty-eighth chartered school authorized by the California State Board of Education. It was also the first authorized in the San Diego Unified School District and San Diego County.

While CSSD was identified as a start-up chartered school, it was actually part of a state program called Education Clinic Alternatives, which was created to stem the tide of public school dropouts within San Diego and other parts of the state.

THE TWO TYPES OF CHARTERED SCHOOLS IN CALIFORNIA

California has two chartered school models: (1) conversion chartered schools and (2) start-up chartered schools. Conversion chartered schools were originally traditional public schools. A start-up chartered school has no history of being a traditional school. From the start, it is established as a chartered school.

CSSD's transition from a district-dependent program to a full-fledged chartered school is the story of a passionate and committed cadre of educators, businesspeople, and community supporters. And now, two decades later, the chartered school movement in California has increased from an initial cap of one hundred chartered schools to over twelve hundred that serve well over half a million students.

From their inception, chartered schools were designed to be a hybrid institution: On the one hand, they would uphold the educational social contract. They would also be subject to oversight and held accountable to ensure students were learning and teachers were maintaining professional standards. On the other hand, chartered schools were encouraged to experiment and innovate to develop new ways of inspiring students to learn and reach their greatest potential. They were also designed as a way for teachers to establish small schools that would bring educators together who shared a common mission. Teachers could actively collaborate with parents to create a student-focused learning environment.

Chartered schools meet their ambitious objectives by a system of governance that is different from that of traditional public schools. Of the forty-three states that authorize chartered schools, each one has its own set of rules guiding how they are created and governed. Since their inception, chartered schools have gained significant ground in communities where they have been established. This separate set of rules gives chartered schools the ability to implement new methodology, make decisions quickly, and adapt to change—all of which were difficult to accomplish within the heavily bureaucratic, regulated, and politicized traditional public education system.

In chapter 4, "Pushback Part 1," we will explore the governance and compliance differences between chartered schools and their traditional public school counterparts, why they played an essential role in the original design of chartered schools and are still relevant today, and why these fundamental differences are the topic of the most heated debates regarding the role of chartered schools within public education.

Rise of the Consumer's Voice: Parents Vote with Their Feet

Before chartered schools, "market-driven" was a term reserved for the world outside traditional public education. This term described how supermarkets, telephone companies, airlines, gas stations, and other businesses operated. No doubt, parents are consumers in a market-driven economy. But for most of public education's history, the institution has maintained a relative market-share monopoly. Thus, the vast majority of parents throughout the country had one option for public education: the nearby neighborhood school.

While private schools have played a role in K–12 education, the small numbers of students they serve mean they have never posed a large-scale threat to traditional public schools. But with the emergence of chartered schools, an increasing number of public school parents have shifted their allegiance. The most high-profile examples of students enrolled in chartered schools in the 2015–16 school year are as follows:

- New Orleans: 92 percent

- Detroit: 53 percent

- Washington, DC: 45 percent

Since 1992, 6,900 chartered schools have been established that enroll nearly three million K–12 students. In the ten years leading to the 2016–17 school year, enrollment in chartered schools nearly tripled, making them the fastest growing form of school in the United States. And in many

US cities, chartered school enrollments are approaching 20–25 percent or more of district students.

According to the California Department of Education, for the 2016–17 school year, California had 1,248 operating chartered schools that educated more than 602,000 students. The outcomes for ethnic minorities enrolled in chartered schools are better than those in traditional schools. For instance, in 2013, 19 percent of African American and Latino chartered school students were accepted into the state's flagship public university system, the University of California, compared to 11 percent of black and Latino traditional public school students. These positive results point to the power of choice. When given the option, millions of parents across the country have opted for chartered schools. Today, consumers are making educational decisions for their children based on schools that are welcoming, academically engaging, and safe.

On a national basis, however, only one in sixteen children attends chartered schools. When it comes to overall market share, the total number of students enrolled in chartered schools pales in comparison to those attending traditional public schools. This low percentage also reflects the limited number of communities that have chartered schools. And where they are present, they frequently are filled to capacity and maintain waiting lists.

Chartered schools have provided parents educational choices that align with the market-driven decisions they make in other aspects of their lives. With chartered schools, parents are able to choose the educational environment that best aligns with their children's needs. While this market-driven framework has fueled the growth of chartered schools and empowered parents in a way never before seen in the United States, it has also threatened traditional public schools' hegemony.

Maintaining the Status Quo: Pushback against Chartered Schools

Throughout our country, public schools receive the majority of their funding through student attendance. For instance, in California, school districts are required to comply with the Local Control and Accountability Plan (LCAP). This is a school district's three-year strategy for how it will use state funding to serve all students. Under current LCAP funding, a school district receives about ten thousand dollars per year for each student. Traditional public schools have maintained a monopoly on this essential revenue source.

In school districts where chartered schools have been established, their long-standing income-generating source has been put at risk. Given that a geographic area a school district serves has a specific number of students, traditional schools have found themselves competing with chartered schools over the same population of students.

The popularity of chartered schools has resulted in decreased student enrollment in traditional public schools. This is compounded by changing demographics in the United States. As the general population contracts, K–12 enrollments have decreased in states and cities across the nation. Increased immigration in some parts of the United States has helped mitigate the overall impact of population decline. Otherwise, the effect of the reduced enrollment in those areas would be devastating.

Empty classroom seats mean less revenue. And less revenue means schools must reduce their teaching staff and increase class sizes. School districts may also be forced to cut spending that may result in decreased facilities maintenance and school services, employee layoffs, and even the sale of school properties.

For the first time in their history, traditional public schools are having to consider market-driven principles such as supply and demand, market share, competition, public relations, and marketing in order to address lower enrollment. But rather than adjust to how chartered schools have changed the public education landscape, school districts across the country are engaging in the practice of pushback in order to maintain their stronghold on per-student funding. Broadly speaking, pushback is primarily a response by superintendents, school boards, central offices, unions, state organizations, and other groups to either slow or stop the growth of chartered schools. Their objective is to hold on to the students within a traditional school's boundaries, stop the flow of students from a traditional school's campus, and maintain the status quo.

The status quo is how those within the educational establishment conduct the business of education on a daily basis. It comprises written and unwritten belief statements that are the result of learned behavior—traditional and past practices that are a school district's efforts to maintain certain long-standing and previous practices; the way those within the educational establishment see how schools fit within the broader US landscape; policies, procedures, and educational code; and the process by which school districts must maintain continual growth in order to remain solvent.

Wherever chartered schools are growing, pushback is occurring. On the moderate end of the pushback spectrum, pushback is a calculated effort to slow chartered schools' growth and expansion. On the extreme end, it is an effort to destroy whatever threatens the educational status quo. In chapter 4, "Pushback Part 1," we will further explore pushback and the status quo, why pushback is becoming increasingly aggressive, and how it is interfering with the objectives of those who have tirelessly labored to improve public education in the United States.

Pushback may be demonstrated by a variety of behaviors. Authorizers may attempt to micromanage the operation of the chartered school. Many school districts may require that chartered school governance mimic the rules and principles districts follow. (Most chartered schools operate under corporate law. Many school districts operate under education code.) Authorizers may be reluctant to approve new chartered schools. Authorizers may place unreasonable expectations for the renewal of chartered schools. Chartered schools often experience inequitable funding, reluctant support in their effort to seek facilities, or a threat of revocation.

A Point of No Return

A strong national defense and healthy international trade will do little for the socioeconomic and political future of the United States without a well-educated citizenry prepared to strengthen our communities on both a micro and macro level. No doubt, the future success of our nation relies on fulfilling the educational social contract. If we equip young people to be self-sufficient adults, informed voters, and productive citizens, we will revive the essential community resources and landmarks that were once left to decay under apathy and neglect.

Whether your perspective is that public education is in sharp decline or merely in transition, you will agree that, because our nation's future depends on a well-educated citizenry, the responsibility of public education is both significant and overwhelming. While parents across the country have sought to enroll their sons and daughters in traditional public schools that meet their children's needs, as our investigation has revealed, many traditional schools have either benignly or blatantly neglected the communities they are funded to serve. This is especially true in our nation's urban centers, areas with a high concentration of ethnic minorities, and socioeconomically disadvantaged regions.

With the introduction and rise of chartered schools, parents have a new market-driven public education model that is academically and fiscally accountable, innovative, flexible, and ready to meet the needs of communities that have been underserved by traditional public education. While misinformation and misconceptions about chartered schools have resulted in their being labeled as harbingers of doom that represent the weakening or even demise of public education, as you have learned, from their original design and onset, chartered schools have always been part of the public education system.

Chartered schools represent the best of what a dramatically changing public education landscape has to offer. At the same time, the chartered school model is still in its early stages and is continually evolving and improving. Unfortunately, pushback threatens the very strength of the original design of chartered schools: to experiment and develop new ways to operate and to inspire students to reach their greatest potential.

Despite often aggressive resistance by those grasping the status quo, chartered schools are a permanent part of public education. In the chapters that follow, you will learn how chartered schools benefit students across the country and have provided parents the peace of mind they seek. You will also gain an understanding of why chartered schools are necessary to fulfill the educational social contract, are worthy of respect and protection, and should be provided the resources and support to improve and grow.

Chapter 2

DAVID AND GOLIATH

IMAGINE YOU ARE a powerful leader. Your enemy has set up camp near you. To your distress, his army is bigger and stronger than yours, full of fearless fighters—and they are ready to battle against you.

Your adversary gives you two options: (1) surrender without resisting, and you and your soldiers will become his subjects, or (2) send your strongest soldier to fight to the death in a duel. If your man wins, your enemy will concede defeat, and his army will become your subjects. If his man wins, your army will serve a new master.

"Because I'm feeling extra generous, I'll give you forty days to decide if you want option one or two," your rival tells you.

You are sent into full panic mode as you scramble to figure out what to do.

Your enemy's fiercest soldier pays you a visit twice every day: once in the morning and once in the evening. "Have you made your decision yet?" he asks each time.

His booming threat matches his over-nine-foot-tall frame and easily crosses the no man's land between you and your enemy's soldiers. They call him Goliath. The warrior is a bona fide giant protected by nearly two hundred pounds of battle-tested, head-to-toe armor.

The pressure builds inside you. Your decision will affect the lives of thousands of people. But no one in your army, not even your most decorated soldier, comes close to rivaling Goliath's might. This means the second choice will nearly guarantee the death of your best warrior. But if you give up and opt for the first choice, you will live a life of regret for not at least trying.

As each day passes, your soldiers become increasingly restless. Word spreads quickly about the options you have been given. Your soldiers are filled with fear of a lifetime of enslavement and begin questioning your ability to lead. As their leader, you are charged with acting decisively and in their best interest. So what's taking you so long to make your decision?

One day, out of nowhere, a young man approaches you and offers to fight Goliath. You size him up and immediately recognize his societal status by his humble clothing. He's a lowly shepherd with no military background. You tell him to go away.

"I've been tending to my father's sheep," David says. "Whenever a ferocious lion or bear takes livestock from our flock, I fearlessly go after the beast and rescue my animal from within its clenched jaws. When it turns on me, I grab it by its hair, strike it, and kill it. Just as I've done to lions and bears, I'll do to Goliath."

Desperate for solutions to the biggest dilemma of your life, you find relief in his confidence. With defeat all but inevitable, you decide to accept his offer and tell your adversary to prepare for the duel.

You dress David in the best armor in your arsenal. The bulky gear is both too heavy and too cumbersome for the young man's slender frame. He refuses to wear it.

"I'll fight him with what I know best: my staff, my sling, and five stones," David says.

The day of the duel, David walks to a brook and collects five of the smoothest stones he can find and slides them in his modest shepherd's bag. He faces Goliath, who is incredulous that he's going to battle with the unarmored young man.

"Do you think I'm just a dog, that you come at me with sticks?" he asks David. "Come here, and I'll give your flesh to birds and wild animals."

"You come against me with sword, spear, and javelin. But this day, I'll strike you down and cut off your head," David says.

Enraged by David's hubris, Goliath rushes to attack him. David reaches into his bag, places one stone in his sling, and masterfully launches the rock directly into Goliath's forehead. It instantly pierces his skull. The giant falls face down on the ground.

The ancient story of David and Goliath teaches us how to deal with obstacles and use what seem to be weaknesses to our advantage. As Malcolm Gladwell describes in his blockbuster book, *David and Goliath: Underdogs, Misfits, and the Art of Battling Giants*, the young man abruptly changes the rules of engagement and through his boldness, saves his people, the Israelites, from Philistine conquest. The biblical account is particularly relevant to the current struggle between the education reform movement and the educational establishment. In this chapter, we will explore aspects chartered schools have in common with David as they boldly challenge the educational model of traditional public schools.

Who Are David and Goliath?

The educational reform movement's version of David comprises a bold, resourceful group of early chartered school pioneers who sought to create a new model of public education. They defied the conventional wisdom of the educational establishment armed with decades of policy, practice, and resources. They fearlessly challenged the traditional public school monopoly over educating our nation's K–12 students.

Today, David the Israelite represents the people, along with their advocacy and passion, within the educational reform movement. These include teachers, parents, and community members. They are bolstered by the principles of change, which include a firm belief in breakthrough pedagogy and a market-driven approach to public education. Their only desire is to operate their educational programs successfully and within defined capabilities, hoping for moderate growth over time.

Traditional school districts and authorizers often represent the educational establishment's version of Goliath the Philistine. Public education's Goliath is often characterized by a refusal to compromise. This inflexibility is largely a result of decades of maintaining a public education monopoly unchallenged. Under this entitled status, change is viewed as both unnecessary and a threat to business as usual. With the growth of chartered schools, the educational establishment realized its monopoly and moral authority could be challenged and even dismantled. Pushback became the weapon to slow and even eliminate the educational reform movement's objectives. Sadly, the resources, energy, and time committed to pushback often come at the expense of delivering high-quality education to K–12 students.

On the one hand, Goliath is armed with a large staff and budget. He often serves as authorizer, signaling a massive conflict of interest when it comes to his desire to maintain his dominance and his power over David. Goliath also often limits David's potential when it goes against his interests. Goliath has been the dominant force for decades and views himself as benevolent and entitled to maintain his top-dog status.

On the other hand, David has limited personnel and resources when compared to Goliath. David is at the mercy of his authorizer, who has the power to revoke his charter and shut down his operations. When Goliath falters, his schools rarely, if ever, will be forced to close their doors. In other words, one of the darker benefits of maintaining a monopoly is a self-policing accountability system that often falls short of objectivity and, in the case of schools, parents' expectations.

When Goliath sees David earning the loyalty of parents and the community, this chips away at his monopoly. In order to remain financially solvent and educationally relevant, Goliath needs to retain his students and gain those he has lost to chartered schools. While an individual chartered school may not have directly harmed Goliath, Goliath sees all chartered schools as harmful and therefore deserving of pushback. Because of this adversarial relationship, rather than work with David to educate K–12 students, Goliath views him as his adversary.

While chartered schools were initially designed as public laboratories that would help traditional public schools innovate, the relationship has devolved from this lofty starting point. Unless traditional public schools are forced to work under an authorizer–chartered school relationship, they have operated independently, always looking out of the corner of their eyes to their opponent with suspicion and distrust. Although they are both public schools, they have developed their own local, state, and national organizations that have served to protect their respective interests. And while both seek market share, broadly speaking, their approaches are different.

Goliath is steadfastly holding on to the monopoly he believes is his right. Within his arsenal, he has multiple pushback weapons, which will slow and stop chartered school growth. David realizes the fastest path to growth is through earning parents' trust. Gaining market share will come through providing students a superior pedagogical product. A culture of independence, innovation, and creativity enables chartered schools to deliver outstanding outcomes. Chartered schools have demonstrated that adversity can be a strength—more is less in this case. Being far smaller and having fewer resources compared to the traditional public school juggernaut has compelled chartered schools to become more creative in their drive to thrive in a challenging environment, call into question the status quo, and earn market share. While pushback has resulted in an adversarial relationship between David and Goliath, Goliath has maintained the upper hand through his seemingly endless funding sources. Time will tell how this relationship will evolve.

The educational reform movement seeks to transform public education to an extent never before seen in history. Chartered schools in the aggregate seem to fall short in size and resources compared to the traditional public school behemoth. But as you will read in the next section, looks can be deceiving. As with David, their smallness may not be the weakness it seems to be.

The battle between the educational reform movement and the educational establishment has been compared to Armageddon, where the two will fight to the finish. While a war of existential proportions may be an overstatement, the battle between the educational establishment and the educational reform movement is no doubt one of the most significant paradigm shifts within publicly funded institutions today.

The Strong and Powerful Are Not Always Strong or Powerful

Chartered schools sought to improve public education through developing an agile, client-centered, focused system. David's strength was, in part, his nimbleness. Goliath's size and armament were what both the Israelites and Philistines viewed as his greatest strengths. In fact, Goliath was convinced that David's small stature and lack of resources would guarantee his defeat.

Many of those at the forefront of the educational reform movement initially believed the educational establishment would welcome innovations developed within chartered schools in order to improve traditional public education.

On the one hand, traditional public schools viewed chartered school innovations with suspicion, skepticism, and hostility. On the other hand, they freely and unapologetically adopted practices pioneered by chartered schools (such as online and blended learning) while rarely, if ever, acknowledging the source of these innovations.

In addition, traditional public schools interpreted the inherent smallness of chartered schools as a sign of weakness. In fact, smallness can be a strength. While traditional public schools have massive resources, their size and complexity prevent them from quickly responding to the needs of students, parents, staff, and the community at large. In maritime terms, steering a supertanker in a new direction is much more difficult than changing course in a nimble speedboat.

Traditional public schools initially viewed chartered schools in somewhat faddish terms: They were an educational trend that would fade away into obscurity or create a minor distraction at worst. Meanwhile, the pioneers of the educational reform movement saw chartered schools as a revolutionary force that would bring about much-needed change within public education. From the start, educational reformers were passionate and confident and had a clear vision they sought to execute.

The educational reform mind-set is dramatically different from that of the educational establishment. Educational reformers have an entrepreneurial outlook. Creating something out of nothing has been the hallmark of self-starters throughout our nation's history. Establishing a nontraditional public school requires courage, open-mindedness, a willingness to eschew safety and embrace risk, and a steadfast faith in the promise of educational reform.

In order to fully execute their vision and reach their highest professional potential, educational reformers must be provided a public school landscape that encourages them to thrive, grow, and innovate. They must be unfettered by unnecessary bureaucratic hurdles that are often the weapon of pushback rather than legitimate regulation intended to improve student outcomes.

The majority of those within the educational establishment have an institutional outlook. They are faithful to the individuals and entities that represent traditional public education. The educational establishment embraces safety and tradition. When new traditional public schools are established, they rely on the same template that has guided public schools for generations. Challenging the status quo is anathema, and change is viewed with skepticism and often outright hostility. Those within the educational establishment are reliant on an entire bureaucratic infrastructure to guide and support them. The mere thought of unplugging from the institution is, for the most part, inconceivable.

As was the case between the mighty Philistines and the inferior Israelites, the educational establishment did not ever anticipate that tiny and insignificant chartered schools could threaten and even overtake traditional public schools.

Similarly, the educational establishment has scale and nearly limitless resources at its disposal. While educational reformers have fewer resources, they are not as entrenched in establishment dogma and are able to quickly adjust to change. As the burgeoning chartered school movement has demonstrated, the public education status quo is both vulnerable and far from invincible.

How Did the Rules of Engagement Change?

David leveraged his strengths, which most perceived as weaknesses. In Goliath's case, he became complacent by blindly pledging allegiance to the status quo. In the end, his underestimation of a small opponent, hubris, and miscalculation cost him his life. Similarly, educational reformers are dramatically changing the rules of engagement. Traditional public schools have a parochial mind-set that values establishment insiders and views outsiders cautiously if not derisively. To create lasting change within public education, chartered schools manage and operate their campuses differently than traditional public schools. Through their innovative programs, they have had remarkable student outcomes and have gained widespread public support. The breakthrough pedagogy that has improved the lives of K–12 students is in high demand from parents. Losing student market share is terrifying to traditional schools that took their monopoly as a given and, through choice and bureaucratic shackles, are not able to adapt quickly to a changing educational landscape.

From the beginning of chartered school history, no one within the educational establishment ever perceived one person or a collection of like-minded individuals would launch a new type of public school. This prototype of the larger chartered schools has a corporate organizational structure, whereas the educational establishment is entrenched in hierarchy, protocol, and the employees progressing from one career stage to the next.

According to the establishment perspective, constructing a public school requires an institution with multiple bureaucratic layers. You need building, curriculum, and oversight departments. But chartered schools and their adventurous leaders eschewed the educational establishment paradigm and proved it was not an infallible and indisputable dogma. Educational reformers had a vision and the courage to execute it. This new model empowered a generation of forward-thinking individuals ready to take on the challenges of public education. By embracing private-industry approaches that were once the bailiwick of entrepreneurs, not public schools, educational reform leaders have brought about unprecedented change and innovation to public education. For example, it inspired an experienced teacher of one school serving a small student population to rise to become a CEO of a multiple school-site system, one that has served thousands of students and posed a threat to traditional public education through delivering outstanding and widely recognized academic outcomes.

The following chart depicts many of the key differences between traditional public schools and public chartered schools. These differences are a result of policies, practices, and procedures supported by state codes or laws. Public chartered schools are granted operational freedoms intended to create an educational environment conducive to creativity and innovation. Our goal for the reader is to examine both columns recognizing the opportunities each structure presents.

CHARACTERISTICS	TRADITIONAL PUBLIC SCHOOLS	PUBLIC CHARTERED SCHOOLS
Organization	Mostly independent, characterized by a bonded interest between county office and neighboring districts.	Independent, characterized by a loose collaboration among chartered schools.
Compliance Framework	Follow all traditional education codes.	Follow corporate law and some portions of traditional educational codes.

CHARACTERISTICS	TRADITIONAL PUBLIC SCHOOLS	PUBLIC CHARTERED SCHOOLS
Source for Facilities	Have traditional facilities provided.	Limited facilities, many of which are self-funded. Limited overhead costs: operate in storefronts, office buildings, and small campuses in facilities that may be leased, rented, or purchased through self-funding.
Teachers' Organization	All union.	Union or nonunion.
Pedagogical Model	Follow traditional model with some variations.	Innovative and creative with no central instructional model.
Schedule	Traditional school schedule.	Flexible schedule.
Technology	Slow to adopt technology due to bureaucratic hurdles.	Easily able to adopt latest technology.
Leadership	Traditional educators have similar backgrounds and experiences. For the most part, leaders pledge allegiance to the institution.	Charter leadership comes from diverse backgrounds that bring fresh perspectives not entrenched in institutional allegiance.
Boards	Elected school boards.	Varied board structures.
Oversight	Multiple levels of oversight through county, state, and federal laws.	Chartered schools are empowered to make decisions based on research and data. They are accountable to authorizers, state law, and federal regulation as called out for chartered schools.
Curriculum Organization	Massive instructional programs and curriculum supplemented by their extracurricular programs.	Limited curricular and instructional programs based on each one's specific educational program.

CHARACTERISTICS	TRADITIONAL PUBLIC SCHOOLS	PUBLIC CHARTERED SCHOOLS
Impetus for Change	Limited to respond only to programs funded by the state and county.	Chartered schools are empowered to make decisions based on research and data. They are accountable to authorizers, state law, and federal regulation as called out for chartered schools.
Boundaries	Teach students within set geographical boundaries.	No school boundaries.
Pushback Level	Subject to little to no pushback.	Subject to tremendous pushback.
Laws	New laws mainly clarify existing laws.	New laws reduce independence and create barriers to entry often driven by pushback.
Support Network	Has a proactive support structure for school boards, superintendents, principals, teachers, and classified staff.	Support by state and national organizations for chartered schools may be classified as moderate to weak.
Student Population	Fixed student population.	Recruited student population.
Identity	Long-standing identity and reputation.	Uncertain as sustainability and longevity remain a work in progress.
Opposing Viewpoint	Districts see chartered schools as subservient to their authority.	Chartered schools see traditional public schools as their equal.
Marketing	Marketing almost nonexistent.	Marketing is a major effort.

Throughout most of traditional public education's history, the major issues the institution faced were based on policy, practice and procedure, and funding. The onset of chartered schools brought about new challenges that changed the rules of engagement for public schools. Traditional public schools were now confronted with a new type of public school that siphoned their primary revenue source—the students within their boundaries. The educational establishment has responded with aggressive pushback, confident its authorization will quickly force chartered schools to back down. But chartered schools have not acquiesced. In fact, they have defended their steadfast students-first values. While district authorizers have viewed chartered schools as essentially serfs obligated to serve their feudal lords, chartered schools consider themselves public education equals. This is based on legal grounds. Under federal and state statutes, traditional public schools and chartered schools are Local Education Agencies, which means both have equal legal standing.

We estimate the educational establishment will require a decade to clarify its rules of engagement with chartered schools. In ten years, we will have a generation of school administrators who know of a public education environment as only where traditional public and chartered schools coexist. They will understand the important role and function chartered schools play and be far more inclined to understand their benefits.

Currently, school districts across the nation are losing market share to chartered schools and are scrambling to figure out how to stop the bleeding. The educational establishment has two choices: attempt to squash chartered schools like a bug under a shoe or take a more moderate and conciliatory approach and direct their efforts toward having chartered schools operate more like their traditional counterparts. We believe the latter approach will prevail. With that stated, we strongly believe that any oversight and operational method must allow chartered schools to maintain their independence, which is one of the greatest strengths of the chartered school model.

In addition, as chartered schools have grown and earned the legitimacy that is their right, philanthropists have taken notice. Powerful benefactors have expressed strong interest and support in the promise of educational reform. Many have shared their largesse with chartered schools, making the movement stronger than ever.

More Is Not Necessarily Better

The chartered school leaders are comparatively small organizations that often have on-site CEOs, who are directly involved in decision-making for an individual campus. While chartered schools are smaller, they have repeatedly demonstrated they can deliver quality educational programs that meet or exceed what giant traditional public schools offer. The greater number of programs traditional public schools have may allow for more flexibility in scheduling classes for students and more options. But many of these classes may be scripted instruction developed by a curriculum coordinator rather than an innovative program tailored to meet the particular needs of a school's students. Whereas the organizational structures necessary for significant innovation and change are often nonexistent in traditional public schools, groundbreaking innovation and change are the goal and hallmark of chartered schools.

During our research in Massachusetts, we witnessed a scenario that perfectly demonstrated the power of independence. Cape Cod Lighthouse Charter School is a thriving school that lacked a proper outdoor play area for its students. One day, the principal's secretary looked out her office window and saw a contractor using his massive machinery to repair a city street in front of the school. She walked up to the contractor and asked if, once he wrapped up the street repair, he could level a rocky field in the back of the school so the students would have a place to play. As the saying goes, "Ignorance is bliss." The school secretary made the simple appeal not knowing the immense amount of work required to fulfill her request or how even doing so broke the educational establishment's compliance and bureaucracy-driven protocol dictating the decision-making processes for its campuses.

To the secretary's delight, the contractor generously obliged. Apparently, the contractor did not know how traditional public schools approved or rejected projects such as these either. Over the course of a few weeks, he and his team moved tons of dirt and rock, and they went on to build the chartered school a playground that included a soccer field. The contractor performed this work for free as a service to the school.

The major project that started with a school secretary's simple request created a playground within a time frame unheard of under the rules dictating construction within the traditional public education system. In Cape Cod Lighthouse Charter School's case, the secretary took it on herself to explore construction options to meet the school's needs. From there, the school's CEO, who worked on-site every day and knew, on an intimate level, the school's needs and goals, gave the green light to move forward with the playground construction. As a CEO, he had the authority to approve, coordinate, and assign tasks.

Cape Cod Lighthouse Charter School's playground project demonstrates the agility that does not exist in traditional public schools. Similar to Cape Cod Lighthouse Charter School's playground project, chartered schools across the country can quickly implement new programs, procedures, and policies. They can adopt new curriculum and instructional methodology guided by staff and teacher recommendations.

Imagine a similar scenario playing out in a traditional public school. Even if the contractor volunteered to donate his time and resources to the school, the site administrator would not have the authority to approve the decision. Rather, it would have to be made at the district level, where administrators would be required to follow a long list of policies, practices, and procedures. This red tape includes school-site councils, coordinators, directors, district administrators, and the planning and building, maintenance and operations, finance and accounting, legal, education, advisory, and athletic departments. With so many layers of bureaucracy, it is no surprise why change occurs at a snail's pace within traditional public schools. This is why even the mere thought of building a new playground within weeks on a traditional public school campus (from approving the plans to having kids play on it) is unheard of.

Instead of multiple layers of protocol requiring meetings, agendas, and endless collaboration, chartered schools are designed to efficiently make decisions and adapt to change. At the same time, when it comes to decisions that require working with school districts, chartered schools encounter the same bureaucratic headaches that traditional schools must deal with. As anyone who heads a small chartered school can attest, sometimes dealing with the layers of decision-making required between the chartered school and the traditional district can seem like trying to scale an insurmountable wall.

The inherent organizational differences between chartered schools and traditional public schools result in both models addressing the same problem and solving it in completely different ways. In many cases, traditional public schools find themselves frozen in a dizzying maze of bureaucracy. In contrast, chartered schools often have efficiently solved the problem and are moving on to address the next challenge.

Those within the educational reform movement are risk takers and are steadfast in the belief that public education as the educational establishment has defined it needs to improve and be completely overhauled—especially in areas where K–12 students are appallingly underserved. The chartered school reformers are challenging the status quo by establishing public schools that break from the educational establishment's expansion model. In fact, professionals within the establishment are typically indoctrinated into its ecosystem. Many teachers and administrators have attended K–12 public schools and have received teaching and administrative credentials from public universities. Most professionals that have become administrators in the system taught in public schools before moving outside the classroom and into the district office. In this closed system, traditional public school teachers and administrators conform to an organizational system that is entrenched in tradition and bureaucracy.

Countless frustrated traditional public school teachers and administrators have fantasized about establishing or working at their dream school, a magical place that addresses all the public education weaknesses they have identified. But moving beyond daydreaming and toward starting up a school is out of the question. Doing so would break with everything they have learned that public education is. This explains why few in the educational establishment can perceive deviating from standard practice in a significant way.

Enter the pioneers of educational reform. Seemingly out of nowhere, a group of highly motivated and talented individuals decided to launch schools that broke from the educational establishment model. The majority of those within the educational establishment had no idea that change of this magnitude was on the horizon.

The pioneers of educational reform developed chartered schools slowly and methodically to bring their plans to fruition. They did not have unrealistic expectations thinking they could offer a one-size-fits-all solution to address the greatest challenges facing public education. Their major objective was to introduce choice through market-driven public education.

Survival of the Fittest

This term implies that those who are best prepared will overcome and experience long-term success. Within the context of the educational reform movement, survival of the fittest is not a fad, nor is it temporary. For chartered schools to thrive in the future, they must focus on building strong fiscal resources and reliable instruction, understand the origins of the educational reform movement, develop a specific mission, and determine how they can complement and collaborate with the educational establishment.

In fact, unless a new and unprecedented collaboration arises between chartered schools and traditional public schools, both may be damaged in the long term. Only the strong will survive, which are public schools that have a solid fiscal and instructional foundation. In this section, we will address the three battles playing out between the educational reform movement and the educational establishment: (1) fiscal viability, (2) public support and trust, and (3) new human capital.

Fiscal Viability

Educational reformers realize the challenges of a market-driven approach. By being its biggest proponents, educational reformers realize they must consistently deliver exactly what parents need. Otherwise, they will lose market share to their competitors. Educational reformers understand they must constantly earn public trust in order to survive in a free marketplace, and they embrace the challenge.

In regions across the country with a large chartered school presence, including cities with the nation's biggest public school districts, traditional public schools are struggling to adapt to a competitive public education marketplace. They are used to operating under a monopoly that allows them to continue being the sole public education provider, regardless of how poorly they perform. Year after year, buildings open their doors in the fall, students attend classes, and teachers show up every day. No matter how much they underperform, schools and their districts always want more funding. Budgets never decrease, and the educational establishment presents the same argument every year: "Our expenses are higher; we need more to survive."

Across the nation, state departments of education, based on findings from the county education departments, have identified districts likely to become insolvent in the near future. The most egregious examples are New York City Public Schools (NYCPS) and Chicago Public Schools (CPS), both of which are more than one billion dollars in debt. These schools teetering on collapse demonstrate the weaknesses of the public education monolith.

Unless chartered schools monumentally shift their strategy by becoming stronger and more organized, they will succumb to educational establishment pushback.

Public Support and Trust

Market-driven public education is a students-first approach. When parents and their children have a choice, they will continually seek out the best public schools possible. Chartered schools providing quality education will be in high demand. Those schools that have planned wisely and followed strategic plans focusing on quality and long-term growth will most likely flourish. Charter management organizations (CMOs) that follow sound business management principles and deliver strong instructional programs could become the most prominent voice of the movement. As a result, they could emerge as leaders whose public school model becomes the vision for all chartered schools. CMOs comprise politically savvy leaders whose influence could drive educational reform.

The chartered school movement is about twenty-five years old. Initially, chartered schools invested in developing a mode of operation that effectively connected parents, students, and school staff. Within a short period, chartered schools have experienced extraordinary growth. From a small cottage industry, they have expanded into multi-million-dollar organizations. Many chartered school back offices rival those of sophisticated private-sector corporations. While book dealers, curriculum designers, turnkey technology companies, professional development trainers, real estate developers, lawyers, consultants, and advisors of every type once focused their marketing efforts on traditional public schools, they are now seeking business opportunities with chartered schools. Chartered schools are mature organizations trusted by the communities they serve and sought after by the private sector.

New Human Capital

Chartered schools have exceeded all expectations, even those of their founders. They began as a small collection of campuses mostly comprising fewer than two hundred students. Today, hundreds of chartered schools exist. Large ones enroll two thousand, ten thousand, and more students. Many are fully mature organizations that bear little resemblance to the scrappy start-ups that landed on public education shores.

The golden age of educational reform has just started as the pioneers and the founders of the movement are reaching retirement age. The future carries with it many variables, including what lies ahead for the growing and vibrant movement, how chartered schools will maintain innovation and independence while shedding their fledgling status and building a well-established infrastructure, what will become of this infrastructure that has supported a growing and vibrant movement, and, most importantly, who will influence and lead the movement—in other words, who will be crowned the Davids of the future.

Throughout the first decade of the chartered school movement, the founders of the movement helped design, develop, and pass charter school law and established the first chartered schools. We refer to these founding leaders as the "originals." The originals had remarkable qualities and skills, including passion, dogged dedication, boldness, and an understanding of student-centered public education instruction. Coupled with experience, a commitment to teamwork, and high levels of expertise, they poured the foundation on which all chartered schools are built. Tomorrow's chartered school leaders must uphold these same values for chartered schools to continue to thrive and defend themselves against pushback. They must be given the freedom to remain centered on instruction and the needs of pupils and families.

At their outset, chartered school leaders needed the skills to launch start-up schools. Staffs at this stage were small and relatively easy to manage. But as chartered schools have grown, they have become complex organizations that require advanced leadership expertise. While, on the one hand, this growth demonstrates the success of chartered schools, on the other hand, chartered schools must always hold to their mission of innovation and independence, regardless of how successful they become. Thus, with growth comes the challenge of maintaining the vision of the educational reform movement.

New leaders must have the management skills that exceed those necessary at the start-up phase. They must have expertise in organizational management, compliance, legal issues and concerns, governance, public relations and marketing, human resources, maintenance and operations, facilities acquisition, legislative analysis, and a strong understanding of the greatest challenges the educational reform movement faces. Today's chartered school leaders must be well trained in educational leadership.

Their skill set must strike the balance between a high-level chartered school's administrator and a corporate leader. Leaders' capabilities must move beyond business acumen. They must be able to meet students' needs, which is part of any successful instructional program. For this reason, those who manage and operate chartered schools must be comfortable with their learning communities. They must be skilled in community outreach.

As the story of David and Goliath has taught us, survival of the fittest does not mean the strongest and most powerful will win the battle. Nor does it mean those who uphold tradition and the status quo are the best equipped to thrive in the long term.

Within public education, the particular rules of engagement between chartered schools and traditional schools vary from state to state and city to city. In Denver, there is a general openness and collaboration between the two. In states where the educational establishment aggressively uses pushback, each chartered school must be prepared to confront that and defend itself by investing in strong instructional programs, financial resources, and outreach, which will earn trust and gain much-needed support from community members.

In addition, chartered schools must hire and retain talented and resourceful staff members. Chartered schools' high-quality staff wind up with high-quality outcomes. Chartered schools must also focus on the similarities they share with successful private-sector corporations. In order for these similarities to continue to benefit chartered schools, their leaders must maintain a hands-on approach to managing their campuses, an openness to change, an insatiable appetite to learn and grow, and constant collaboration with the greater educational reform movement.

Leaders that combine sound business principles with the particular needs of public schools are best equipped to take on the greatest challenges their schools face. An ability to leverage the strengths of the private sector is one example among many that demonstrate why chartered schools must fight for their independence and freedom.

Chapter 3

MYTHS

ONCE IT IS full steam ahead, changing a ship's direction is no easy feat. When a captain decides to alter an ocean liner's course, it takes an astonishing level of engineering and power to steer the vessel in a new direction. Take, for example, the mechanisms that steered the *Titanic*, which was the world's largest ship during its time. Its rudder measured nearly eighty feet high, weighed more than one hundred tons, and was cast in six separate pieces. To move the massive rudder itself, engineers installed two steam engines. The ship had three propellers: two had a twenty-three-foot diameter, and one had a seventeen-foot diameter. The combined horsepower of its engines was fifty-one thousand.

Traditional public education, similar to all large organizations, has a *Titanic*-like aspect. While some within the educational establishment may realize public schools need to change course to meet the needs of a rapidly changing educational landscape, the sheer size of the bureaucratic behemoth makes quick changes in direction impossible.

In fact, for the most part, public schools embrace their decades-old traditions and culture. They are proud of their institution. This mind-set often values the status quo over change, which is frequently viewed with skepticism and downright hostility. In and of themselves, tradition, culture, and the status quo are not inherently negative. The problem arises when a blind allegiance to these values or a narrow-minded perspective fails to address the most pressing problems public education faces today.

When student outcomes are dismal and parents maintain reasonable expectations and crave better for their children, then public schools must eschew old models. If preserving and growing public education fail to put students' needs first, then the educational establishment is prioritizing self-interest over the public good.

Chartered schools have signaled a seismic shift within public education. Educational reform movement pioneers have boldly challenged the status quo, especially in instances when it has unequivocally failed students. Rather than uphold tradition and culture as infallible public education ideals, educational reformers have embraced innovation. Instead of viewing the status quo and the institution as inviolable, educational reformers are eager to introduce a new market-driven model of public education.

Within a short period, chartered schools have embarked on a new journey, untethered to the massive traditional public education juggernaut. By being fiercely independent while still working under the umbrella of public education, chartered schools have acted with an agility unheard of within traditional public education. It is this agility that has given chartered schools the ability to innovate. And in communities across the United States, innovation has resulted in outcomes that have far exceeded those of traditional public schools.

Rather than embrace the breakthrough practices chartered schools have developed, the educational establishment has largely held a tight grip on the wheel and has steered its ship in the same old direction. What chartered schools offer is largely rejected and viewed as a threat to the sacrosanct status quo. Pushback is a weapon used by the educational establishment to maintain its top-dog status. Its purpose is to slow, if not stop, the educational reform movement, which aims to bring about a market-driven approach to public education. Too often, however, rather than preserving students' best interests, pushback is a heavily funded and finely tuned weapon of mass distraction, one that keeps traditional public schools from taking a deep look inside to solve its biggest problems.

There are several myths about chartered schools in persistent circulation. Unfortunately, chartered schools' relatively small size in comparison to the titanic size of traditional public schools means dispelling misconceptions about chartered schools is much harder to do on a national level. While not explicitly and directly promulgating lies about chartered schools, the educational establishment only gains from negative public perception of educational reform.

Anyone who has worked within chartered schools is familiar with myths associated with them. Many of the perspectives, based on inaccurate information, seem to be concerned with a particular school, located in a specific city and within the boundaries of a certain school district and neighborhood. But on further examination, the myths clearly target both local chartered schools and the educational reform as a nationwide movement.

States and school districts themselves are given significant control over how they run their schools. Because the educational reform movement started at the state level, the history and development of chartered schools is rooted in the individual states that have established charter school law. In other words, chartered schools launched and evolved differently from region to region. Furthermore, the particular circumstances within a state have influenced and will continue to influence how chartered schools develop within that state.

Despite the diverse histories of chartered schools across the country, they have been plagued by similar myths. In our cross-country research, we found wherever the school was located, its leaders expressed similar frustrations regarding common falsehoods. In other words, most attacks against one chartered school are actually common to all chartered schools. Those armed with erroneous information were usually vociferously opposed to chartered schools. Unfortunately, presenting accurate information often does little to diffuse myth makers' sometimes irrational hostility toward educational reform.

In this chapter, we will set the record straight. We will dispel the most common, incorrect, and damaging myths about chartered schools. And we will present the truths that demonstrate how chartered schools are a shining example of public education fulfilling its promise to improve the lives of students across the nation.

Why Do Chartered School Myths Persist?

Prior to the internet age, community members learned about their schools by the following means:

- The observations family, friends, and neighborhoods made about them

- The news they read in the local publications, such as the performance of high school teams and athletes

- What they observed when they drove past a local school, including its appearance and student behavior

While these methods still play a significant role in influencing public perception of chartered schools, the internet has transformed how we gather information and form opinions. Online, you will find endless content, both accurate and inaccurate, about chartered schools. If you are looking to strengthen your bias against chartered schools, you will discover articles, blogs, and social media content that will confirm your perspective.

Unfortunately, for those of us at the front lines of the educational reform movement, countering fiction with fact is not easy. The myths about chartered schools have persisted. One significant reason is most adults attended K–12 traditional public schools or private schools. This is the system of education they know best, and chartered schools are outside their personal experience.

Furthermore, in comparison to students who have been educated through traditional public or private schools, the population of students who have matriculated in the chartered school system is much lower. Also, because of their smaller size, legislation and laws regarding chartered schools are much lower profile and lesser known than those relating to traditional public schools.

Last, the education reform movement, while growing every year, is significantly smaller overall than the educational establishment.

But as chartered schools increase market share across the country—expanding in states that have charter school law and opening doors in states that will have charter school law—they will play a larger role in the national discourse about public education. Already, chartered school success stories are making local and national news. Hollywood films and critically acclaimed documentaries have been produced about them. Politicians highlight them in their campaign speeches. And family members and friends have their children enrolled in them or work for them or both. As the footprint of chartered schools grows, their higher profile will give educational reformers the platform necessary to dispel myths and provide accurate information to increasingly wider audiences.

What Are the Chartered School Myths?

The following are common myths associated with chartered schools. People claim they:

- are private schools;

- cherry-pick students;

- operate with minimal oversight;

- are not held accountable for academic performance;

- are an unproven experiment;

- do not accept English-language learner or special-needs students;

- use public funds but are not held academically or fiscally accountable;

- take money and control that should go to traditional public schools.

In the following section, we will address each myth.

MYTH: Chartered Schools Are Private Schools

In a 2014 Phi Delta Kappan (PDK)/Gallup poll, respondents were asked if chartered schools were public schools. Almost half—48 percent—of respondents said no. Unfortunately, this myth that chartered schools are private schools is one of the most harmful to the educational reform movement. Chartered schools are public schools—they always have been and still are today.

Because chartered schools are public schools, they must be free and accessible to all. In other words, they cannot charge tuition, and they may not have selective admissions. Also, chartered schools have open enrollment, which means all public school-age children are eligible.

With that said, significant differences exist between chartered schools and traditional public schools. One significant difference is a majority of states have laws that absolve chartered schools from a major portion of local-district policy and procedure. For example, in most cases, chartered schools are not bound by a collective-bargaining agreement.

The myth that chartered schools are private schools fuels widespread fears that they will take over public education. Because chartered schools are public schools, such spurious claims are both misleading and inaccurate.

MYTH: Chartered Schools Cherry-Pick Students

In just about every state we visited, school district staff believed chartered schools consider admitting only the best students. "Cream of the crop" and "cherry-picked" were terms often used to describe this practice. Sometimes they cited the "oversubscribed" approach. This means, in the lower grades, the chartered school enrolls more students than it can easily accommodate. From first to eighth grade, students who cannot handle the workload and rigor leave the school. This narrows a school's enrollment, so by grade eight, the classroom is populated by the highest achievers.

Do all chartered schools practice "creaming," cherry-picking, and oversubscribing? No. Although some schools might try to recruit the best students, it would be difficult to accomplish. Keep in mind that, in most states, chartered schools are required by law to conduct a lottery when applications exceed the number of seats available. Because chartered schools are public schools, they must be free and accessible to all. They may not have selective admissions policies. Doing so would be in violation of charter law.

In fact, in some states, such as California, chartered schools serve a large number of at-risk or lower-achieving students. Fair and balanced research shows that chartered schools enroll students with varying aptitudes and diverse backgrounds. The bottom line is that chartered schools reflect the diversity of the community. In fact, when viewed on a large scale, they are incredibly diverse.

MYTH: Chartered Schools Operate with Minimal Oversight

This myth is based on the following premise: Chartered schools are independent corporations; therefore, they operate without the same oversight of their traditional counterparts. This myth is easily dispelled. *Chartered schools must operate within the provision of state and federal law.* They cannot discriminate on the basis of race, color, sex, or national origin.

Chartered schools are overseen by authorizers. In fact, the term "charter" refers to the contract document that outlines the formal agreement reached with the authorizer. The authorizer has the responsibility to hold the chartered school accountable to follow charter law. Authorizers review financial records, conduct audits, determine if the chartered school may be renewed, and if found to be noncompliant, have the option of non-renewal. Chartered schools are in fact so highly monitored in terms of instructional outcomes, operational process, and financial accountability they are often held *even more accountable* than traditional public schools. Think of it this way: If a chartered school is found out of compliance with charter law, the authorizer can shut down its operations. Countless examples of traditional public schools behaving badly have made headline news. Yet, despite their underperformance year after year, they continue receiving taxpayer dollars and keep their doors open.

One reason this myth persists is chartered schools operate at least in part as corporations. This is a new model for public education. Their organizational structure provides chartered schools the independence that has resulted in the innovative practices that are their hallmark. The educational establishment is not used to this new model of public school organization. As you learned earlier, tradition, culture, and the status quo are frequently elevated to sacred status within traditional public education—even if they are not serving students' best interests. The educational establishment views the organizational structure of chartered schools as both foreign and a threat to its public education monopoly.

The chartered school's governing board is the body vested with the responsibility of seeing that the school is open and accountable to charter law. This governing board is also subject to various business regulations, ethical financial practices, and open meeting laws. Far from operating under minimal oversight, chartered schools must adhere to rules established in their charter and set by their respective state regulations.

MYTH: Chartered Schools Are Not Held Accountable for Academic Performance

Chartered school operators have grown in sophistication since the 1990s. Similarly, authorizers have grown in their understanding of chartered schools and how they operate. In the early years, when chartered schools began the journey toward their major role in making a difference for students, authorizers were preoccupied with chartered schools' fiscal and operational workings. Taking care of a chartered school's viability seemed to those monitoring them as the single most critical step in guaranteeing a school's compliance with charter law.

When chartered schools proved skilled at managing their charter operations, authorizers turned to monitoring for quality. Today, most authorizers have criteria for renewal that includes a strong academic component. Chartered schools must reach an established academic standard in order to assure their charters are renewed.

Everyone involved in the education of young people agrees on one thing: Educational programs of every kind should be able to demonstrate they are high quality and students are learning. But what constitutes "high quality," and who decides if the chartered school's instructional program demonstrates an acceptable standard for high quality? Chartered school pioneers are working to answer just that.

Quality measurements are now considered reasonable and appropriate for decision-making concerning chartered school educational practice. Multiple data points are becoming for many an integral part of high-quality, data-driven support. Many experts representing both traditional public education and chartered schools strongly believe that high-stakes assessment data are not an appropriate means for making categorical judgments about an instructional program. The multiple factors affecting the results of high-stakes assessment data also mean these tests provide important but limited information. After all, multiple aspects contribute to a school's quality, many of which are not quantifiable in one standardized test.

For example, a high-stakes test does not accurately measure parents' satisfaction level with the school's outcomes. A standardized test does not demonstrate if parents believe their children are safe, motivated, self-confident, working toward post-secondary education, and generally flourishing in an environment that is not teaching to the test. One test will not explain why a chartered school consistently has a long waiting list. Solely using a single assessment as a means to hold a school accountable is an oversimplified and inaccurate measurement tool.

Authorizers are now considering multiple measures. They realize one piece of data cannot tell the whole story. At the high school level, attendance, graduation rates, grades, credits earned, credit recovery outcomes, college readiness, and career education preparation are all measurements worthy of consideration. Elementary and middle schools have other measures that signal success. Evaluating a school using multiple measures is a far more comprehensive approach that considers the particular needs and differences within the various levels of K–12 public education.

Chartered schools are rigorously assessed and reassessed. The criteria are evolving, as is the need to explore various models for evaluating chartered schools. For example, states with only a district's board of directors charged with evaluating progress are often considered to operate from a self-serving, biased position. This is why districts are infamous for functioning in an unsupportive manner where chartered schools are concerned.

The National Alliance for Public Charter Schools and many state-level associations, such as the California Charter Schools Association (CCSA), strongly advocate for chartered school accountability and standards that demonstrate quality by using multiple measures. At the same time, they also recommend vesting the authorizing of charters to entities other than local school districts. This will remove conflicts of interest that stem from school districts seeing themselves operating in direct competition with the very chartered schools they are evaluating.

From the start, chartered schools have been held accountable for the performance of their students. This is in their self-interest, and to thrive, they must meet—and exceed—accountability standards. Well-performing chartered schools provide the strongest foundation for public support and continued growth.

MYTH: Chartered Schools Are an Unproven Experiment

Chartered schools quickly moved from an experimental stage to one firmly based on practices that bring positive results. For example, very shortly after their creation, chartered schools were largely responsible for developing online and blended learning. It did not take long for district personnel to see the value of these new delivery methods, confirming the benefit of chartered schools' experiments. This is another instance of the power of independence and how it encourages chartered school innovation.

The extraordinary growth of chartered schools over the past decade, as well as long student waiting lists for many chartered schools, suggests that chartered schools have moved far beyond any experimental stage. Their success—seen as chartered school market share continuing to threaten the educational establishment's monopoly over public schools—establishes chartered schools as solid alternatives to traditional public schools.

While some school district leaders and their staff have remained open-minded and have sought to learn from innovative and successful chartered school practices, moving the educational establishment ship is an unenviable task. Unfortunately, these examples of embracing chartered school innovation are the exception rather than the rule. With that said, groundbreaking delivery approaches developed at the chartered school level are now considered acceptable practice within traditional public schools and chartered schools.

Experimentation continues within aspects of chartered schools, as it should. Trying different methods, textbooks, schedules, and so on opens doors to improved education, which can benefit students in all schools. But chartered schools themselves long ago left the experimental stage and now are unquestionably providing quality education to all levels of students.

MYTH: Chartered Schools Do Not Accept English-Language Learner or Special-Needs Students

A persistent and inaccurate misconception is that chartered schools have the option to accept or reject special education and English-language learner students. Contrary to popular belief, throughout its history, the educational reform movement has been at the forefront of serving these students.

For English-language learner students, the vast majority of chartered schools' student populations reflect the composition of their traditional public school counterparts in most subgroups.

For special education, many school districts relied on chartered schools to teach the special education students within their boundaries. Before pushback became the weapon of choice against chartered schools, districts determined it was more cost-effective to send their special education students to chartered schools, and they gladly did so. Fast-forward to today, and both traditional public schools and chartered schools across the country follow the same state-mandated special education requirements.

Even in cities where district data themselves indicated chartered schools enrolled special-needs students at an equivalent rate as traditional public schools, critics still maintained chartered schools sidestepped their commitment to special education students. Some schools do report as few as 1 percent of their students are special education. But no solid evidence indicates chartered schools as a whole underserve the special education population. In fact, a great deal of data indicates that some chartered schools serve more than their fair share. For instance, in San Diego, the School for Entrepreneurship and Technology (formerly Coleman Tech Charter High School) reported more than one-third of its enrollment in 2016–17 as students with disabilities or as English learners.

There are, however, means for monitoring consistently low special education enrollment and then instituting needed changes. For example, the El Dorado Charter SELPA in California, sponsored by the El Dorado County Office of Education, is one of the first of its kind. Approved by the California State Board of Education, it serves as a prototype for a creative means of chartered schools working to deliver quality special education services while maintaining reasonable costs per student. El Dorado Charter SELPA monitors special education data carefully and investigates any statistics that appear questionable. Likewise, renewal regulations in most states require that chartered schools demonstrate they are delivering equitable services to a broad range of subgroups.

No doubt, chartered schools equitably serve students that reflect their community's demographics, including English-language learner and special-needs students.

MYTH: Chartered Schools Use Public Funds but Are Not Held Academically or Fiscally Accountable

Chartered schools not only are held accountable academically and fiscally, but they also are held to higher standards than traditional schools.

In order to foster innovation and creativity, chartered schools are granted flexibility when it comes to instructional delivery, governance, administration, and business application. With that said, chartered school authorizers are required to develop clear and fair standards of academic and fiscal accountability.

As chartered schools increase their profile within the K–12 educational landscape, they are held to a higher level of public scrutiny. And if a chartered school fails to meet academic or operational expectations, an authorizer may decide to not renew or to revoke a school's charter, which means a chartered school can be shut down. Even the most poorly performing traditional schools are often protected from closure.

For example, Arizona has an A through F grading system for all schools. Charters that receive an F are frequently closed. Traditional schools with an F grade have a process for closure, but it is much more difficult to execute than the process for chartered schools.

State legislatures prepare charter law. The state's board of education outlines regulations that govern the implementation of that law. Local granting agencies develop a process that governs chartered school oversight. The strength of the policy, regulation, and process depends on collaborative efforts of all those who prepare and implement chartered school policies. These efforts must always include the chartered school operators and community. Those writing and executing policy should support mutually arrived-at standards and practices that govern the operation of chartered schools.

As you will read throughout this book, the fundamental differences between chartered schools and traditional public schools logically require that chartered schools be held to a separate set of academic and fiscal standards. In other words, a one-size-fits-all approach to accountability, where both chartered schools and traditional public schools follow identical standards, will most likely present more problems than solutions.

Regardless, the myth that chartered schools are not held accountable academically and fiscally has no basis. Not only must they meet such standards required of traditional public schools, but chartered schools also must often exceed those levels.

MYTH: Chartered Schools Take Money and Control That Should Go to Traditional Public Schools

Chartered schools' greatest critics claim chartered schools siphon money and control from the local district, thereby forcing it to reduce services and furlough, lay off, or permanently release teachers. This myth promotes the concept that school districts are losing revenue to chartered schools. As a result, their schools become inadequately resourced thanks to a rogue public school that has come to town. Chartered schools, in the minds of district staff, unreasonably capture dollars that should be flowing directly from the state to the district or county office. The idea that education funds follow the student does not compute within the public school establishment's deeply biased point of view.

When a school district's enrollment declines for whatever reason, the district has a very difficult time reducing the size of its footprint. And when enrollment drops dramatically year after year, this spells disaster. Any business entity knows that to survive, its infrastructure must be in line with changes in its environment, such as its customer base, labor market, economic conditions, innovations, and more. Whether growing or shrinking, a business must always adapt to change. People are employed, wages are set, and operations are adjusted based on what is needed to continue to serve the client base. In a monopoly, however, no one ever thinks of funds following the customer. Under this model, the concept of quality often slips away. After all, when customers can go to only one place for service, the quality of that service becomes irrelevant.

Educational reformers maintain an entirely different perspective. Chartered schools are not taking away the district's money and control. This argument is based on the false premise that funds are the district's from the start. They are not. They are tax-based state funding (which means they are paid for by parents and other residents) directed toward the delivery of a quality education for each student. This is the "money and control follow the student" approach. "Money and control follow the student" implies a fiduciary responsibility on school leadership. They are charged with carefully and wisely serving as the custodians for all funds intended to benefit students and the functions of effective education.

Unfortunately, some school leaders see the money as theirs to spend as they please. But if parents choose an option other than the public school operated by the neighborhood's school district, then the taxpayer-generated state education funds should be expended on behalf of the student—regardless of which public school a student attends.

The educational reform movement believes that parents should play the biggest role in deciding the best environment for their children's learning experience. They, rather than bureaucrats, have the greatest interest that their children be enrolled in safe, secure, welcoming, motivating, inspiring, and challenging public schools. All students deserve an educational setting in which they gain a love of learning. Too often, however, they have functioned as a cog in a system that is more vested in its self-interest than in that of the students it ostensibly serves.

Chartered schools do take money that would otherwise go to school districts, but these funds should not necessarily go to the traditional public schools. The money should go where the parents believe it best supports their children's education, and in many cases, that is to the publicly funded chartered schools.

Chartered Schools Are Here to Stay

The jury is no longer out. The debate is moot. Chartered schools are here to stay. While some within the educational establishment remain intent on destroying chartered schools, most have largely moved on from this extreme perspective. Yet pushback efforts continue, trying to defend the educational establishment's status quo. Given this situation, the current question becomes: "How will traditional public schools respond to chartered schools, now that they are firmly in the public school mix?"

But does even this question, based on a more moderate stance, warrant further scrutiny? Across the country, we have spoken with leaders within the educational reform movement and the establishment. As a result, we found ourselves challenging the premise of a steadfastly adversarial approach to chartered schools.

Chartered schools were originally conceived as a means of improving educational models for all public school students. They would serve as laboratories of innovation whose breakthrough pedagogy would influence all public schools. School districts, school boards, unions, policy makers, and the public at large would learn from what chartered schools developed. Unfettered by the antiquated policies that discouraged creativity, improvement, and reasonable accountability, chartered schools would benefit all public schools.

At their onset, and as is the case today, chartered schools would innovate by working outside local district policy and procedure. Cookie-cutter policies, as they have come to popularly be known, are policies school boards have implemented and are forced to apply to every school within its jurisdiction. Often, these policies make little sense, especially in large and diverse urban districts such as Los Angeles, New York City, Chicago, and Detroit.

What chartered schools have demonstrated spectacularly well is that governance best serves a learning community when it is focused on that community's specific needs. When governance and strategic planning are local and free to function in a manner that puts students first, the following benefit: instructional practice, fiscal priorities, operational management, training and development of personnel, and all other essential elements associated with creating schools that are safe, motivating, and inspiring.

Self-preservation, self-interest, and politics may never be completely removed from the public educational landscape. But the accountability of a school's governing team, whether democratically elected or appointed, will be more transparent and accountable when it is not lost in the muck and mire of huge bureaucracy, one so bloated and entrenched that any activity oriented to making even a minor change is akin to turning a massive ship.

In regard to trade unions, in and of themselves, they are not a deterrent to change within public education. But their often-relentless insistence on compromise limits everyone involved in teaching and learning. Union forces are powerful, and in places such as California, they truly serve as one of the biggest obstacles to change. In other states, a more collegial relationship exists. Schools, communities, teachers, administrators, and parents work together to make a difference in the classroom, whether traditional or chartered.

In most states, chartered schools have been offered a choice. Some are affiliated with unions, and some are not. The difference with chartered schools is that those campuses selecting a union environment demonstrate a willingness to work with the union. Where collaborative relationships based on trust exist, improvement and professionalism flourish. This is a win-win scenario.

Although chartered schools are here to stay, what remains to be seen is the extent and force of educational establishment pushback. Will those in opposition to any change categorically reject challenging the status quo? We certainly hope not. In fact, we remain optimistic. As fierce as pushback is, we hope the educational establishment will choose open-mindedness to isolation, change to holding on to the self-serving status quo, and teamwork to obstruction. We look forward to the day when the educational establishment will embrace the groundbreaking work of chartered schools and acknowledge their contribution to public education.

Thanks to the tireless work of educational reformers, chartered schools have emerged as a hothouse of ideas that offer what every parent, administrator, teacher, school board member, and legislator really wants to see in his or her local public schools: a publicly funded and well-functioning education system that works for all students—one that leverages precious tax dollars every family pays to provide a world-class learning environment.

In the end, the onus of myth busting rests on all of us within the educational reform movement. It is every chartered school advocate's duty to cast out these myths and shed light on the stellar example of the promise of educational reform.

In the era of the *Titanic*'s fateful maiden voyage, massive ocean liners sailing in icy waters regularly encountered and even collided with icebergs while successfully completing their journeys. This in part explains why, despite receiving multiple warnings of drifting ice from other ships, the *Titanic*'s captain continued full speed ahead in the Atlantic's freezing waters. By the time a lookout spotted the massive iceberg, it was too late for the *Titanic* to change course.

Similarly, those at the forefront of educational reform are today's public education lookouts. Without a doubt, chartered schools have far less market share than the traditional public school monolith. But in this case, chartered schools' smaller size is a strength. With smallness comes agility. Without a doubt, the educational establishment could benefit from the agility of chartered schools. Like tugboats pulling ships many times their size, chartered schools could guide traditional public education through challenging waters.

Chapter 4

PUSHBACK PART 1: AN OVERVIEW

As president and CEO of The Charter School of San Diego,
Mary Searcy Bixby is a member of Vistage.

VISTAGE IS A global networking group comprising CEOs, executives, and business owners. Being part of Vistage means I'm fortunate to be surrounded by smart, successful, and highly motivated people. During our monthly meetings, we share sound business practices and support one another. We also take turns presenting an issue within our respective organizations, relying on our peak-performing colleagues to provide input regarding how to solve a particular problem.

When it was my turn to put forward an issue I was seeing within my industry, I sought my colleagues' insight regarding the tipping point, which describes an evolutionary marker at which a system reaches a significant and irreversible development. The concept was made popular by Malcolm Gladwell, who wrote a best seller of the same name, and it is often associated with the epidemiological phenomenon of an infectious disease reaching a point where it spreads uncontrollably. Seeking input from my colleagues, I asked them, "What percentage of market-share loss signaled a tipping point in your organization?"

Through the investigation Tom and I had conducted of schools across the country, we had encountered major school districts experiencing substantial losses in student attendance as a result of the growth of chartered schools. This could spell fiscal disaster for traditional public schools. We believed having a frame of reference outside public education would help us answer this question, which is why I sought my Vistage group's input as to what percentage of losses signaled a tipping point for their companies.

Previously, you read that students enrolled in chartered schools have reached 92 percent in New Orleans, 53 percent in Detroit, and 45 percent in Washington, DC. These examples are far from exceptional. Big school districts throughout the country are losing significant market share to chartered schools.

We knew the risks districts faced when they lost high numbers of students. The greatest of these was a sharp decrease in revenue because a district's primary source of income is based on student attendance. What we did not know was the specific percentage point at which the effects of decreased school enrollment would be irreversible to a school district's long-term viability. In other words, what was the attendance-attrition tipping point for schools throughout the nation?

Prior to receiving my colleagues' responses, Tom and I came up with our own tipping point projections for the businesses my Vistage colleagues represented. Considering we saw losses as high as 84 percent in the public school sector, we guessed 20–30 percent would be a conservative estimate for companies.

When I presented the 20–30 percent range to my colleagues, the eyes of every single one of them grew large. Several turned to each other to see if the person sitting next to them was equally as shocked by what I had just said. I immediately knew Tom and I had missed the mark with our estimate.

"Mary, you might be a little off on your data," Mark said diplomatically, breaking the group's silent disbelief.

Mark is Vistage's chairperson, as well as my executive coach. He had built his successful career as an entrepreneur in the financial services industry.

"Well, if it's not 20–30 percent, what is it?" I asked.

"If a company reaches a 3–4 percent loss, it has serious concerns on its hands," Mark said.

The other business leaders concurred with his observation.

Mark explained that maintaining profitability was a company's biggest responsibility—running in the black was expected and red was unacceptable. Thus, if a company's market share dropped by as little as 3 or 4 percent, it would signal a possible crisis, and crisis mode would require immediate action. A business leader would take a deep look inside the organization to identify where the company had gone wrong and how to reverse the market-share loss. He or she would restructure the company's strategic plan and marshal its fiscal and human resources to change course. The business leader would scrutinize the company's labor force, how it delivered its product or service, and the overall reasons that clients were jumping ship and buying from competitors.

When I told my Vistage colleagues about the double-digit market-share losses Tom and I witnessed in many of the nation's most important and high-profile school districts, they were incredulous—they were probably as shocked as I was to hear their 3–4 percent figure. The bottom line is the market-share losses we saw in districts across the country would spell disaster for any of the companies my Vistage friends ran. They would probably be forced to declare bankruptcy, lay off all employees, and perhaps even close down for good.

Most school districts experiencing substantial decreases in market share due to chartered school enrollment have not reacted with a response that comes even close to what profit-seeking businesses do. If parents are exiting the system, then this is a sure indication of crisis. But for years, it seems as if school districts have largely conducted business as usual, seemingly oblivious to devastating losses within their organizations. But, as you will read in this chapter, complacency on the part of those within the educational establishment has turned into pushback, a result of the undeniable consequences the tipping point has had on traditional public education.

A Tipping Point Guide for Traditional Public Education

The tipping point is a phenomenon that appears in biological and human-made realms. In the context of public education, the tipping point is the loss or threat of loss of market share that will result in permanent or long-term disruption to a school district's status quo, which you learned about in chapter 1 and is a concept we will explore in greater detail in this chapter. The following is a visual guide demonstrating how the tipping point applies to traditional public education.

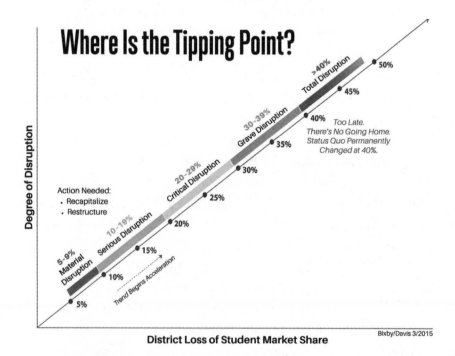

District Loss of Student Market Share

Bixby/Davis 3/2015

The chart we developed relies on observations of schools and school districts, research, and interviews. Rather than based on statistical analysis, the chart reflects our evaluation of traditional education.

We welcome those interested in public education to continue to analyze the effects of the tipping point on school districts and their campuses. The conclusions, we believe, will be the same as ours or at least similar.

Six Variables That Influence a District's Tipping Point

There are multiple reasons different school districts will experience total disruption at various percentage levels. This is because school districts are complex organizations that are highly regulated by state and federal law. Thus, the tipping point for one district will be different from that of another. In other words, based on our observations, no specific percentage of student market-share loss signals a tipping point that will apply to all school districts.

At the same time, in the most extreme cases and based on our observations, a 40 percent market-share loss due to the presence of chartered schools will have a dramatic effect on a school district's mode of delivery and operations. With such a loss of market share, even if school districts absorbed all chartered schools or states drastically changed their charter laws about governance and funding, districts would most likely never be able to return to business as usual.

The following are diverse and complicated variables that influence a school district's tipping point (we will explore each):

- Leadership
- Finances
- Workforce climate

- Demographics
- Community change
- Political climate and operational needs

Leadership

In the context of traditional public schools, leadership comes from state legislators, city mayors, community leaders, school boards, superintendents, media representatives, parents, school-site staff, and other individuals and organizations. But out of all these individuals, on a day-to-day basis, the superintendent has the biggest impact on a school district. In particular, a school district's success or failure often depends on the quality of the superintendent's leadership. Thus, leadership plays a significant role in determining whether the district is heading toward its tipping point and, if so, how quickly it will reach it.

Multiple leadership characteristics of a superintendent influence the decisions he or she makes. Three, however, have an especially strong impact on a school district's success. Whether they are superintendents, small business owners, or CEOs of Fortune 500 companies, all effective leaders demonstrate **openness**, the **ability to work with others**, and **a clear vision of their role**.

First, **openness** is essential when it comes to skillfully adjusting to change, which is inevitable in any organization. A superintendent's ability to maintain an open mind allows him or her to identify change and embrace it when appropriate. With this receptive attitude, the superintendent is able to evaluate the consequences and benefits associated with a particular change and how to best adapt to it in a timely fashion. In addition, openness comprises the following qualities: honesty, trustworthiness, approachability by others, receptivity to criticism, and willingness to consider alternatives.

In contrast, a superintendent with a closed-minded perspective is unable or refuses to see the signs of change and adapt as needed. This will cause the district to fall behind broader trends in public education. Over time, he or she will be increasingly unable to exert effective control and, through continued resistance, will threaten the district's long-term interests.

Unfortunately, clinging to past practices (even if they are effective) or maintaining a tight grip on a narrow definition of public education benefits no one—not even the superintendent that advocates such limited views. His or her general refusal to identify and embrace change increases the likelihood the district will move toward the tipping point.

The second characteristic of effective leaders is the **ability to work with others**. This means directing, compromising, and knowing when to do each.

Often, directing is seen as strength, and compromising is viewed as weakness. But this is not always the case. Effective leaders have developed the leadership skills necessary to determine when to direct, when to compromise, and when to do both. Whichever approach they take, effective leaders demonstrate their power by always maintaining respect for all stakeholders.

An ability to work well with others also means a superintendent values collaboration. He or she listens to other viewpoints, fairly considers alternatives presented, and recognizes others are working toward the same end. He or she knows a key part of evaluating a solution's success is that all stakeholders believe their perspectives are valued, respected, and acknowledged. A superintendent accomplishes this through establishing a respectful working relationship with everyone involved.

From interacting with K–12 students to legislators, a superintendent's ability to work with others is continually tested. His or her daily interactions define the superintendent's overall style and will affect his or her ability to achieve greater goals.

Furthermore, an ability to work with others includes the capacity to motivate a workforce in a positive manner. This requires balancing between insisting the workforce take a specific path and giving them the power to take alternative action when they can demonstrate its benefit.

Leaders that lack an ability to work well with others frequently refuse to cooperate with those who have different views—in particular advocates of change. They see leadership as a power play and winning as a primary objective. Under this paradigm, winning means implementing their agendas, even if they are not in students' best interests. Cooperation and compromise are often viewed as signs of weakness, especially when they require acknowledging perspectives that challenge theirs. Leaders' focus on personal power at the expense of ignoring or rejecting others' contributions only moves the school district toward the tipping point, as they fail to consider ideas that can reverse course.

The third characteristic all effective leaders have is **a clear vision of their role**. When a superintendent looks to the future, he or she considers solutions that may be outside the district's long-standing traditions. At the core of this perspective is a focus on championing the mission and values of the organization. A superintendent who has a clear vision of his or her role always puts students' needs above displays of power.

An ineffective superintendent has a myopic and parochial view of public education. This narrow perspective often comes from a strong desire to preserve his or her power at all costs. Maintaining this leadership style frequently puts the students' best interests at risk. And a superintendent's failure to keep students' educational concerns at the forefront will increase the likelihood the school district will move toward its tipping point.

In summary, highly effective superintendents are experienced and capable leaders. Their openness, ability to work with others, and clear vision of their role separate them from their ineffective counterparts and improve the lives of the K–12 students they serve. Leaders with these qualities are the best equipped to adapt to a changing public education environment.

Finances

While the national spotlight focuses on the country's biggest school districts, such as New York City Department of Education, Los Angeles Unified School District, and Chicago Public Schools, the majority of districts have fewer than five hundred students. This means most school districts are small enterprises. For them, student losses have a proportionately larger impact than they do for larger districts. While five, ten, or twenty students leaving a large school district would not significantly harm its bottom line, such an enrollment decrease could irreparably damage a small school district's operations.

Whether large or small, all school districts must have adequate fiscal resources and reserves to ensure their long-term financial health. The quality and accuracy of a school district's budgeting process varies widely from district to district. A budget's quality and accuracy is also a direct reflection of a superintendent's leadership because he or she is responsible for its oversight.

School districts with a weak budgeting process are consistently unrealistic about their projections regarding the next school year. They may lack accurate and timely data. Their projections may be overly optimistic for the sake of balancing budgets or implementing improvements they actually cannot afford. Overall, poorly executed budgets make a school district unable to effectively address unanticipated events, such as the challenge chartered schools bring to public education's exclusive franchise.

School districts must follow state and federal guidelines, and these provide key insight into the fiscal challenges school districts face. By law, districts must maintain an accurate and timely budget. Districts present their budgets to their county offices of education. If they are out of compliance, they must resubmit a corrected budget.

Regulations also dictate how school districts spend the vast majority of the annual funding they receive. Laws usually restrict a school district's ability to build large financial reserves. Many laws also limit how districts can spend reserve monies. For example, reserve funds may have to be used only for state-approved expenses, such as facilities maintenance, expansion, economic downturns, and repairs associated with natural disasters.

For districts that experience budget shortfalls, administrators and staff are often under tremendous pressure to meet their students' needs with limited resources. Maintaining operations under adverse economic circumstances, such as from market-share losses associated with chartered schools, may leave a school district with little to no human capital. In the end, long-term student enrollment losses can gravely damage a school district.

Overall, school finance is a complicated business. Districts are expected to adhere to strict state and federal guidelines. Unfortunately, the regulatory mechanisms designed to increase accountability can also keep a district from maintaining its long-term fiscal health. Given the work required to comply with the law and meet everyday operational needs, many districts are ill prepared to absorb a loss of students. In these cases, even a minor enrollment decrease could have seriously damaging effects on a district's fiscal health, thereby pushing it toward a tipping point.

Workforce Climate

School districts are complex organizations that are dependent on a highly qualified workforce to support long-term viability. The district's ability to survive—and its health—is reflected in the morale and retention of its employees, instilled in each succeeding generation of employees. In general, the health of a district is strengthened via a workplace in which employees feel safe, appreciated, satisfied with their compensation and benefits, their work conditions are generally positive, and their positions are stable.

The opposite is true as well. A school district's long-term health is at risk when employees feel unsafe, underappreciated, dissatisfied with their compensation and benefits, their work conditions are subpar, and their positions are in danger of being eliminated. Broadly speaking, when a district or school site has a high number of teachers with a negative workplace perception, their attitudes influence the instructional quality they provide. When students receive inferior instruction, parents blame their home school and the district for neglecting to uphold the educational social contract. As we described in chapter 1, the educational social contract states that the purpose of public education is to prepare young people to be responsible citizens, who intelligently exercise their right to vote, become productive individuals, and positively contribute to society.

In districts where teachers are dissatisfied with their workplace and chartered schools exist, parents are more likely to enroll their sons and daughters in chartered schools, thus pushing traditional public schools toward a tipping point.

Demographics

Demographics are the profiles of the students receiving public education. Demographic criteria include gender, racial, and ethnic identity; gifted and talented education, special education, at-risk, or English-language learner designations; social mobility; free and reduced lunch (Title 1) status; school level (elementary, middle, or high school); and the educational level of a student's parents.

School districts that inadequately meet the needs of students that represent particular demographic groups lose credibility regarding their ability to serve their communities. If school districts have chartered schools, parents are presented with options that may better address the demographics of their children. And this enrollment loss may push a district toward a tipping point.

Community Change

In general, housing and community redevelopment directly affect community change. Community members that share similar ethnic or socioeconomic status or both often live in the same geographic area. In order to fulfill the educational social contract, it is incumbent on school districts to identify and serve their students' needs.

Often, when community members have a high level of satisfaction with their public schools, this indicates schools consistently fulfill the educational social contract. But when community members have a low level of satisfaction with their public schools, this typically signals that the school community has failed to meet the educational social contract.

Low levels of satisfaction may be a result of the following: poor safety within a school (such as high incidents of violence, drug use, or bullying); an unwelcoming environment for students and parents; a dearth or absence of college preparatory, Advanced Placement, honors, or International Baccalaureate curriculum; or a lack of specialized opportunities, such as performing arts, STEM, or college and career readiness.

Following are examples of US cities that demonstrate community changes that drive a school district toward a tipping point.

In Detroit, Michigan, and St. Louis, Missouri, public school enrollment has decreased significantly due to large-scale resident exodus. Both cities were once major industrial centers that attracted and supported large populations. But after massive factory closures, the regions' economies stagnated and then shrank and, with them, their K–12 student populations.

Detroit Public Schools (DPS) taught 156,000 students in 2002. But by 2016, that number declined by 70 percent to 46,000 students. As a result, DPS's budget deficit has grown to hundreds of millions of dollars.

During our visit to St. Louis, we met with Robbyn Wahby, the city's deputy chief of staff of the Office of the Mayor. She described that, at the height of St. Louis's industrial boom, the population peaked at 850,000 in the 1970s. An extended period of decline followed. According to the 2013 census, the population was around 318,400, which represents a 62.5 percent decrease. This significant contraction explained why we saw hundreds of abandoned buildings as we toured the city. In fact, as cited by the *St. Louis Post-Dispatch*, across St. Louis, forty-five schools have been vacated.

In Chicago, Illinois, white flight from the city to the suburbs that occurred after World War II led to a precipitous population decline. While Chicago's suburbs flourished, its urban core withered. In 2013, Chicago Public Schools, the nation's third largest school district, voted to close fifty-four of its underenrolled and empty campuses. The district was—and is—buried under more than one billion dollars of debt, and selling its assets is one way CPS has been addressing its fiscal crisis.

The characteristics of the community in which a school is located should drive a district's operations and how it meets its students' needs. In this regard, how a school district addresses changes within a community plays a critical part in determining its tipping point.

Political Climate and Operational Needs

Under most state laws, school board members drive all programs that affect district classrooms. In other words, they shape how districts operate their schools. Thus, the longer school board members have served, the greater impact they have on the district. In addition, school boards approve all budgets. They also make decisions that affect the instructional program, the welfare of its employees, and the general funding of the district.

Traditionally, local, state, and federal politics have highly influenced school districts. Decisions made through politics affect a school district's employees, curriculum, and general operations, so a community's power brokers and stakeholders wield tremendous political power on school districts. Power brokers and stakeholders include elected leaders, successful businesspeople, service club leaders, parents, boosters, heads of community-based organizations, unions, religious groups, and philanthropists. These individuals and organizations are well funded and have a wide sphere of influence. As a result, they have a significant influence on the opinions of the public at large, who are responsible for electing school board members.

Superintendents and school boards benefit when they effectively make shared decisions with power brokers due to the influence they wield. This results in school district employees, power brokers, and other community members fulfilling the educational social contract. And doing so reflects positively on the school board and others in power positions, feeding a positive-outcome cycle.

In some states, one of the most important political relationships is between school boards and unions. A union's goal and responsibility are to advocate for its members' salaries, benefits, and working conditions. When school board positions are up for election, unions will use their resources and influence to support candidates whose views align with their objectives. The relationship between unions and school district administrators plays an important role in how prepared a district is to deal with decreased enrollment due to chartered schools. Often, school districts negotiate high salary increases. School districts are then under pressure to increase enrollment to generate revenue. They often may also be required to reduce expenses by cutting back on resources, which often negatively affects educational services. A significant loss of revenue can place a district in a very vulnerable place. It endangers a district's ability to provide salary, benefits, and a comprehensive educational program and maintain its facilities and operations.

Shrinking student enrollment also influences the political pressure unions and community members place on school boards. When it comes to unions, decreased enrollment in a district may mean staff positions are cut. Fewer staff positions mean a union has a smaller pool from which to draw membership dues. For community members, when a district has decreased enrollment, the public often perceives this as a weakening of their local schools. Community members frequently hold politicians responsible for the health of their public schools. As a result, when a district has decreased enrollment, unions and politicians often wield political pressure on school board members to keep the district from heading to the tipping point.

For a school district to remain healthy, it must have a successful curriculum; a properly funded instructional program; professional development programs; properties that are clean, attractive, and well maintained; a safe and orderly environment; healthy and nutritious meals; and adequate transportation. School districts that lack these characteristics will struggle with providing a quality education to their students. When faced with competition from chartered schools that successfully meet their operational needs, a school district may be pushed to a tipping point.

Tipping Point and Pushback

School districts are charged with maintaining strong leadership, finances, and workforce climates. They must accommodate demographic and community changes. And they are responsible to adapt to the current political climate and meet their operational needs.

A district may succeed in one or more of these areas. But a high degree of competency in all aspects is required for a school district to maintain long-term viability and avoid a tipping point.

All variables are also interconnected, which means a weakness in one area will often negatively affect another. For instance, a school district's fiscal woes will influence its ability to meet its operational needs or provide a workplace in which employees feel safe, appreciated, satisfied with their compensation and benefits, their work conditions are generally positive, and their positions are stable.

The degree to which school districts, superintendents, and others within the educational establishment perceive the tipping point will also contribute to the amount and extent of pushback.

Forms of Pushback

Historically, school districts have, for the most part, maintained a monopoly in education and its options. With the onset of chartered schools, districts are now competing with chartered schools over the same population of students. With 10 percent, 20 percent, and 30 percent losses in market share, districts are having to consider market-driven principles. To address lower enrollment, terms such as "supply and demand," "market share," "competition," "public relations," and "marketing" have entered the public education lexicon.

Under this dramatically changing environment, some schools are adjusting more willingly than others. Those fighting change and rejecting the market-driven principles chartered schools have introduced are doing so through pushback. This response by superintendents, school boards, central offices, unions, state organizations, and other groups to the growth of chartered schools may merely attempt to hold the chartered school movement in line or, at a more extreme level, aim to eliminate chartered schools altogether.

Pushback manifests itself in diverse forms, depending on the interests and intent of its source. It mainly comes from school districts, unions, and local, state, and federal governments. Thus, chartered schools have the unenviable task of addressing pushback from multiple sources.

Regardless of its source, however, pushback aims to hold on to as many students as possible in the traditional schools. Its actions are manifested in the following ways:

- Written and unwritten belief statements

- How their schools fit within the broader US landscape

- Policies, procedures, and educational code

- Solvency through continual growth

Written and unwritten belief statements: These are part of how school districts maintain long-standing practices. Within districts and campuses, written and unwritten belief statements are highly valued and a result of learned behavior at the district and school-site level. They help define and strengthen a district and school's role within a community, including the support they receive from the neighborhood they serve. They are intended to uphold and cherish the quality of a district and school's programs and promote the mentality of always being the best. Written belief statements are embedded within policies and appear in mission and vision statements and mottos. Unwritten belief statements are embodied in a campus's colors and mascot.

How their schools fit within the broader US landscape: Chartered schools are challenging and changing the role traditional schools have played within society at large. For example, one type of chartered high school may have most of its students attend classes online. In this instance, imagine a public high school without a bustling campus, a football field and team, a band, and other markers of a traditional secondary school. Those that identify a high school by these symbols may struggle to understand the diverse forms in which public schools can manifest today.

Policies, procedures, and educational code: School districts strive to uphold and perpetuate their long-standing policies and procedures. They seek to maintain their policies and formulas for funding, hiring, instruction, staffing, and compensation; the physical appearances of their school sites; and their hierarchical organizational structures, which have superintendents at the top followed by administrators and teachers. School districts are also required to comply with state educational codes. Chartered schools are public corporations and operate under corporate law, both of which set them apart from how traditional schools are run.

Solvency through continual growth: Every year, school districts must generate higher amounts of revenue in order to cover rising operational costs. The most common methods of boosting income are through increasing student enrollment and budgets.

Average Daily Attendance and Pushback

With the unprecedented and unexpected chartered school boom, particularly within the past decade and as a result of large charter management organizations, pushback has become a highly organized, well-funded, and aggressive policy. It is fueled by this principle:

Where students go, money and control follow.

In order to understand this key concept within pushback, we will provide a brief overview of how traditional schools are funded. Average daily attendance (ADA) is the foundation of public school funding and comprises the following formula: the total days of student attendance divided by the total days of instruction.

ADA is how states determine how much money a school district will receive for each student it serves. It is also a school district's primary funding source. So without students, a school district would not receive the lion's share of its revenue.

In addition, school districts are required to set their budgets a school almost a year in advance. For example, the 2017–18 school year budget was actually established in early 2017. In 2017, months before the next school year has begun, a school district must forecast how many students will attend its schools. Some states require forecasting to project not just for the next year but also for many years in advance. This formula is largely based on the previous year's attendance. The district must determine how many teachers, administrators, and support staff it will need to educate its students. It has to account for the books, school supplies, and support materials it will purchase for the next school year. Therefore, by the first day of the 2017–18 school year, the district has already invested in students it has projected will attend its traditional schools.

The combination of ADA and budgets set months in advance is an effective funding model for school districts—as long as they can accurately predict student enrollment. Thus, this funding formula's reliability hinges on the district's ability to accurately assess the trends in its area—those related to economic conditions, movement of families in and out of the district, family size, as well as loss of students to nontraditional public schools within its borders. If a school district budgets for a specific level of school enrollment and large numbers of students do not show up on its campuses, the district is now faced with a serious fiscal problem. Herein lies the origin of pushback.

School districts assume the students within their boundaries are solely theirs to educate. According to this perspective, chartered schools are siphoning off resources that school districts believe rightfully belong to them.

> **All school districts believe they are entitled to receive the funding associated with the students within their boundaries.**

Imagine the following scenario: It is fall of the 2017–18 school year, and the school district set up its budget during the 2016–17 school year. A chartered school has recently launched, and due to students applying to it through open enrollment, the school district now has one hundred fewer students on its roster than it had forecasted. In this particular state, the school district receives ten thousand dollars per year for each student. So one hundred fewer students means one million dollars less to pay for everything the school had already budgeted for.

In this district, for every twenty-five students it loses, it must shrink its staff by one teacher. Thus, one hundred fewer students means the district must reduce by four teachers the teaching staff it had previously hired. Fewer teachers typically means class sizes will increase. In addition, the school district has already purchased books, school supplies, and support materials for the one hundred students that have fled to the chartered school. With the unanticipated drop in enrollment, the district now risks running out of money before the school year ends. What this scenario also means is the chartered school has taken one million dollars from the school district. This is because the money the state has available for educating students remains at a specific level, based on the total number of students in state-funded public schools. The total amount is not contingent on which state-funded public school those students attend.

The Political and Economic Impact of Shrinking Footprints

Our nation's major school districts are responsible for managing budgets of millions, hundreds of millions, and even billions of dollars. For example, Los Angeles Unified School District, the nation's second largest district, has an annual budget of more than seven billion dollars. To put this into perspective, this figure is larger than that of many US states. Clearly, with gigantic budgets such as this, school districts are tasked with enormous responsibilities. They must plan for their present needs and project decades in advance in regard to student demographics, facilities, human resources, and more.

To illustrate the complexity of what school districts face when enrollment drops, we will use the seemingly straightforward example of school closures. Let us say a school district has fewer students attending its schools and empty classrooms. One simple step to address significantly shrinking budgets and the high costs of facilities maintenance would be to sell underused or empty facilities. This is a common practice within the corporate world. But for school districts, doing so comes at great political and economic cost.

We will first explore the political repercussions. Consider the consequences of a school district announcing it will close an underused school and generate desperately needed revenue by selling the land. With the backing of their powerful union, teachers at risk of losing their jobs would protest. Angry parents would pack school board meetings. The mayor's voice mail and email inbox would be flooded with incensed voters who would threaten to vote him or her out of office for closing down schools. The media would portray the school board as incompetent, the city's politicians as inept, and the parents as victims of a corrupt and callous education system.

For example, in 2008, former chancellor of District of Columbia Public Schools, Michelle Rhee, closed twenty-three campuses during her controversial and high-profile tenure. (She made the cover of *Time* and was the subject of the PBS news program *Frontline*.) Her move ignited large-scale protests against her leadership. The then-mayor of Washington, DC, Adrian Fenty, also faced political backlash for his outspoken support of Rhee. Fenty's 2010 reelection campaign was viewed largely as a referendum on Rhee's chancellorship. Fenty lost the election, and Rhee resigned from her position shortly after.

Now, let us examine the economic consequences. Suppose that, despite the political fallout, the school district decides to close the campus and sell the land anyway. In the decade that follows, the community experiences a population rise. The district does not have enough schools to educate its students and must build a new campus. But since the last sale of school property ten years ago, real estate prices have risen. Now, the district finds it cost-prohibitive to purchase the same parcel of land it had sold off. This is one important reason school districts are reluctant to sell off underused or empty facilities.

Due to the political and economic consequences of school closures, districts across the nation are reluctant to reduce their real estate holdings.

As Chartered Schools Grow, so Will Pushback

The concept of pushback is new in K–12 public education. For decades, traditional schools worked alongside religious and nonreligious private schools in a largely non-adversarial and nonconfrontational environment.

Traditional schools mostly viewed private schools as a niche that did not threaten their student base. The perspective of the traditional school giant was "there are more than enough students for everyone."

Even with the onset of chartered schools, traditional schools did not view them as a threat to their long-standing monopoly. They believed they would fill a space similar to that of adult education, continuing education schools, and magnet schools, all of which were entities created within the school districts themselves. Thus, chartered schools were not viewed as competing against a school district's interests. In fact, not even those who designed charter school law and established the first chartered schools foresaw their explosive growth—an expansion that has unfolded since their inception.

Pushback is occurring wherever chartered schools are growing and in all states where chartered schools exist. Awareness and fears associated with the tipping point are motivating school districts to aggressively pursue pushback, which is disappointing to parents and those who have tirelessly worked to improve public education. Despite growing and well-funded pushback, the educational reform movement has not backed down. Driven by a passion to put students' needs first, chartered schools have valiantly earned their place within public education. As the saying goes, "Knowledge is power." Chartered schools must continue to stay abreast of the latest tools of pushback to thrive in an increasingly adversarial public education environment and continue to put students' needs first.

Chapter 5

PUSHBACK PART 2: MULTIPLE PERSPECTIVES

CHARACTER COUNTS! IS a popular educational program that school districts across the country have adopted. It comprises a framework for teaching K–12 students the following six ethical values: fairness, trustworthiness, respect, responsibility, caring, and citizenship. Schools that have invested in the CHARACTER COUNTS! curriculum believe the six principles are keys to engendering a healthy campus culture.

The popularity of the program provides insight into the values school districts uphold and believe strongly in. In this chapter, we will explore one of these values: fairness.

When it comes to chartered schools, many districts believe their rise is in large part due to the unfair circumstances under which they are allowed to operate. Districts' pushback is an attempt to create what the educational establishment deems a fairer public education landscape by leveling the playing field. This would effectively deny chartered schools their foundational attributes—their competitive advantage, their ability to innovate and experiment, and their structural strengths—and thus their reason for existence.

Here, we will provide essential background regarding the origins, motivations, and objectives of pushback.

The Rules Governing Traditional Public Schools and Chartered Schools

To comply with state and federal law, traditional school districts must abide by strict policies, practices, and procedures. Each state is allowed to establish its own framework. Over time, this regulatory framework has also become part of each school district's organizational culture. The designation given to these policies, practices, and procedures varies depending on the state in which the district is located. For example, in California and Texas, the state-wide framework is called the Education Code; in Washington, it is divided into the Revised Code of Washington and the Washington Administrative Code; and in Virginia, it appears in the Administrative Code.

In addition, certain states leave individual school districts to establish their own rules, in which case these regulations fall under the board of education's policy, practices, and procedures. To simplify terms, we will call a traditional public school's governing policies, practices, and procedures its compliance framework.

In the case of chartered schools, they are regulated by a different set of rules called charter school law. So far adopted by forty-three states and the District of Columbia, charter school law is written at the state level and mandatory for all states that authorize chartered schools. Similar to the compliance framework governing traditional school districts, charter school laws vary from state to state, and they must comply with state and federal guidelines. According to the Center for Education Reform, strong charter law has several characteristics, including the following:

1. Strong charter law allows for an unrestricted number of chartered schools and students that can attend them.

2. Strong charter law allows multiple charter authorizers.

3. Strong charter law exempts chartered schools from most laws and regulations governing school districts.

4. Strong charter law provides chartered schools with fiscal flexibility.

5. Strong charter law stipulates full funding for chartered schools.

The educational reform movement believes these tenets are essential to establish chartered schools that will succeed. In other words, they lead to thriving campuses that uphold the educational social contract, as well as inspiring learning environments in which an ever-increasing number of schools represent the highest ideals of public education.

The educational establishment believes charter laws that reflect these qualities provide chartered schools unfair advantages that would harm traditional public schools. In the next section, we will explore each point from the perspective of chartered schools and the educational establishment, as well as how pushback, as defined in the previous chapter, manifests itself for each of these five characteristics.

1. Strong Charter Law Allows for an Unrestricted Number of Chartered Schools and Students That Can Attend Them

The Chartered School's Perspective

A market-driven approach to public education is one of the chartered school movement's core strengths. A public education marketplace that offers a wide variety of options empowers parents to make the best decisions possible when it comes to educating their children. When parental choice is the hallmark of a public education system, the needs of children come first. Indeed, the identity of the educational reform movement is rooted in a market-driven approach. Thus, its principles of choice and competition are embedded within its organizational DNA. Rather than viewing it as a disruptive force that must be stopped at all costs, market-driven public education is to be welcomed and embraced.

Unfortunately, the long-standing monopoly school districts have held on public education has led to a system entrenched in bureaucracy and the self-serving agendas of special interests. Over time, both have grown and increased in power, which has resulted in their priorities shifting away from serving the best interests of K–12 students and toward fulfilling their organizational agendas, which include survival and perpetual growth. Examples of this can be found in many large metropolitan cities.

From retailers to tech giants, in a market-driven ecosystem, choice drives the business model. When the public education system moves from monopoly to free market, schools that offer the highest-quality programs, meet parents' needs, and provide the best outcomes rise above their underperforming counterparts. The most competitive schools are rewarded, and those that fail to live up to parents' expectations will either be forced to improve or put their long-term survival at risk.

Those advocating to restrict the growth of chartered schools point to the problems associated with saturation—there are so many schools that there are too few students to fill all the seats available within a given area. Saturation may occur where there is a freer and more open public education market, as when chartered schools are allowed to establish schools within blocks of other educational options.

Regulation in regard to saturation must be very carefully developed and designed. If, in fact, traditional public schools are underperforming, then chartered schools should be granted every right to be placed in their proximity. Authorizers and chartered school leaders should collaborate to determine where to locate chartered schools to avoid saturation when appropriate and to support chartered school success.

For traditional school districts, chartered schools create an unpredict-able variable when it comes to projecting year-to-year student attendance within a district's boundaries. When a chartered school opens its doors, the district may lose tens or hundreds of students to the competing cam-pus. This translates to diminishing revenues for the district, and with less income comes pushback.

The causes of saturation from chartered schools vary depending on a state's charter law. During our meetings with school district officials in West Palm Beach, Florida, they described how saturation has occurred in certain areas that have an abundance of traditional and chartered schools located in proximity. This has contributed to competition among tradi-tional and chartered schools to fill vacancies.

Cases of extreme saturation may not serve students' best interests. According to our investigation, saturation is most widespread in densely populated urban areas, which typically have high degrees of educational inequality. Many families in cities such as Chicago, Los Angeles, Mem-phis, Phoenix, and Washington, DC, are desperately seeking better options than poorly performing traditional public schools. The chartered school growth in these areas is creating a public education surplus, where more seats exist than students to fill them. As a result, all public schools in a given area become underenrolled and therefore underresourced. A simple solution does not exist to address the problem. Increasing gov-ernment regulation to restrict where and when chartered schools can set up shop runs counter to a market-driven approach to public education. The educational reform movement embraces the free-market and pub-lic school landscape that gives a chartered school's board of directors the freedom to realize its vision without bureaucratic red tape.

Nevertheless, saturation is a real problem that can result in an area's chartered schools cannibalizing one another. Since the affected chartered schools are responsible for correcting this problem, we definitely are opposed to any school district's effort to control saturation by regulating any but its traditional public schools. Chartered schools should have the freedom to operate within the boundaries of a granting agency without burdensome regulation that could easily be used as a pushback weapon.

Unless educational reformers determine how to address saturation, indiscriminate growth will result in limited growth. A market-driven approach rewards the public school that produces the best outcomes. At the same time, launching a school is a monumental task. Initially, growing pains are inevitable, and creating an amazing school requires dedication and time. Multiple chartered schools in an area may find they are unable to reach their organizational potential due to the simple fact that there are not enough students to go around. It would be a devastating blow to the educational reform movement if it survived relentless pushback only to succumb to saturation rooted in a gross lack of planning and coordination among chartered schools in a given area.

Thus, it is in the best interest of chartered schools to determine a long-term solution to address saturation. Chartered school operators in saturated areas often argue that their decision to establish a school in a particular area is never indiscriminate and always based on research. But upon further analysis, this research is frequently insufficient.

A chartered school's board of directors must encourage a practical analysis to determine where to establish a chartered school. The following are important questions to consider:

- How many age-appropriate students live in the proposed area?

- What are the three-, five-, and ten-year population projections?

- How many seats already exist within the designated reach of the proposed school? (This question includes seats in traditional public schools and chartered schools.)

- What housing plans might affect the future landscape?

- What are the public education options, and are they successful?

- Do the preceding options draw students easily, or are all the other public education options within a given area struggling to make their student enrollment projections?

- While passion, commitment, and a "failure is not an option" attitude are admirable, is the effort to create one chartered school worth the challenge of driving down the competition?

While saturation is no doubt problematic, it is not categorically harmful. Within a consumer-driven public education system, saturation pushes all public schools to increase academic outcomes and outperform rivals in order to boost market share. In other words, what the educational establishment pejoratively labels as saturation those at the forefront of educational reform call market-driven competition. Whereas the educational establishment views saturation as a threat to its dominance and spends millions of taxpayer dollars pushing back against it, those within the educational reform movement understand saturation's role within a market-driven system, which puts the consumers' needs first, rewards innovation, and punishes complacency.

The market-driven model that has moved our country forward, improved countless lives with inventions and services, and inspired individuals across the world has the power to do the same for public education.

In cities across the country where traditional public schools are underserving students and consistently yielding dismal results, saturation is the jolt these underperforming schools need. It is the call to action to push them out of rampant mismanagement and a culture of failure that has been one of the negative outcomes of the educational establishment's monopoly. In a market-driven approach, public schools are perpetually pressured to boost results to maintain and grow market share. Schools with inferior outcomes will have an incentive to improve their programs to remain viable. Institutions that consistently perform at a high level will attract students and the dollars they bring to the schools they attend. Consider this a "rising tides lift all boats" versus a "race to the bottom" paradigm. In a market-driven public education landscape, complacency is not an option for any school wishing to thrive.

Those opposed to unrestricted chartered school growth point out that saturation can occur on individual campuses, a phenomenon known as colocation. Similar to roommates sharing an apartment, colocation means chartered schools and traditional public schools occupy the same campus. When it comes to colocation, whether the educational establishment agrees with the practice, it is part of the compliance framework in many states.

For example, in California, voters passed Proposition 39, which, according to the California Department of Education, amended the state's public education compliance framework and required school districts to "make available, to all charter schools operating in their district . . . facilities that will sufficiently accommodate all of the charter's in-district students, and that the facilities be 'reasonably equivalent' to other classrooms, buildings, or facilities in the district." Thus, resisting colocation violates the law and spurns democratically enacted legislation mandated by a state's citizens. Chartered schools have won several major court cases against school districts that have attempted to deny them their state-given rights to equal access.

Opponents of colocation frequently neglect to bring up that it is not a revolutionary or disruptive development. For decades, magnet schools have successfully shared facilities with traditional public schools. In fact, school districts across the country strive to have the evidence to be able to boast about the amazing outcomes of their magnet programs. That is, these districts suggest colocation works as long as it meets the self-serving needs of a school district and does not threaten its monopoly.

While chartered schools find themselves fighting for colocation, they do so only when colocation is the sole viable option for a school to secure facilities and open its doors. Chartered school leaders are the first to point out the disadvantages of colocation. The practice is an example of "the lesser of two evils." Chartered schools require facilities to operate. Most would prefer their own dedicated facility.

Similar to a roommate situation, however, colocation can work well only when both parties compromise, treat each other respectfully, and are benevolent to each other. If the shared facility is large enough for two public schools to operate, then the possibility of colocation success increases. But with two sets of administrators, staff, and students sharing one facility, colocation is difficult from the start.

To add to an already adverse arrangement, the educational establishment frequently uses colocation as a pushback weapon. Pushback can be passive-aggressive: A district will do the minimum required to comply with the law but no more. And the facilities it does offer are far from ideal for the burgeoning chartered school. The attitude from school districts often seems, "We'll comply with the law, but you'll have to find a way to exist." But if a chartered school has no means by which it can rent or lease a facility, the school is doomed from the start.

Under some arrangements, a school district can honor a chartered school's request for facilities, but because one facility is too small for the chartered school to run its entire program, the school has no other option than to divide its program across multiple sites offered by the district. In this case, chartered school students clearly are the innocent victims of this practice. Managing one solid public school program is difficult enough on one campus and more so if the school is spread across multiple campuses.

Most states with charter school law have an abundance of surplus facilities. The problem is they may not be in areas close to where a chartered school's prospective students live. For example, the empty school may be in the old part of town that has a low student population and is miles away from a chartered school's target. Because in most cases chartered schools do not provide transportation, this would put the chartered school at a competitive disadvantage when it comes to attracting parents to enroll their children in the campus.

Even if the chartered school considered using an old facility, the upgrades necessary to renovate rundown bathrooms, classrooms, and the overall wear and tear that occurs when a facility has been abandoned could prove cost-prohibitive for a school running on an already limited budget.

The nature of two programs sharing one facility also limits either school in its ability to expand. In some cities, chartered schools find it nearly impossible to find facilities. Boston, for example, has many historic buildings, and its strong preservation laws may make performing renovations necessary to establish a solid program difficult or even impossible. This points to challenges associated with finding suitable property for a chartered school to establish a campus. In many of our nation's urban centers, where chartered schools are often outperforming traditional public schools, securing facilities is difficult for several reasons, including the following:

- Bringing an old building up to legal standards is frequently cost-prohibitive for the chartered school.

- Prospective buildings may be protected under historical preservation laws, which make upgrades either illegal or too expensive.

- Demand for commercial property may exceed supply, which drives up square-foot rental costs.

- In some urban areas, school districts performed cost-benefit analyses and determined building a brand-new facility was more cost-effective than upgrading an existing campus. The old school was virtually abandoned and replaced by the new school. While the previous campus could house a chartered school, bringing the neglected building up to legal specifications is often cost-prohibitive.

Public education is a state function. Therefore, all surplus facilities should be allocated by the state. Currently, however, all property remains under the local school district's ownership.

Chartered schools in need of space often lease underused facilities from school districts. While this should be a straightforward process, chartered schools frequently have to navigate their way through multiple bureaucratic hurdles. For many chartered schools, they feel as if they must beg individual districts for what results in being assigned inequitable and poorly maintained sites that do not reasonably meet students' needs.

Although school districts behind pushback refuse to acknowledge it, a mountain of evidence proves that more chartered schools mean a better public education system. For example, in Louisiana's case, had it not been for chartered schools, the students most affected by Hurricane Katrina would have received no public education during the weeks and months following the natural disaster. In 2014 and 2015, more than one hundred chartered schools served over seventy thousand of the state's students, 82.5 percent of whom were economically disadvantaged.

Allowing an unrestricted number of chartered schools improves the options for all participants. As in an open-market system, competition leads to innovation, more real choice, and better opportunities for customers—for chartered schools, students, and parents. If saturation results, schools wanting to survive must respond, just as in the free market. Although dealing with saturation can be a painful process for some schools, in the end, students and parents will benefit.

The Educational Establishment's Perspective

The unrestricted growth of chartered schools challenges the long-standing monopoly traditional school districts have had on teaching the students within their boundaries. As you read previously, the budget a school has set for one school year is actually developed and approved during the previous school year. Thus, a school's ability to establish an accurate budget is largely based on being able to project the number of students that will fill its seats the next school year. The educational monopoly gives school districts an ability to reasonably gauge the following year's student population because the district knows most students will attend its schools from year to year. Well-managed budgets are key to a district's ability to fulfill the educational social contract.

Still, districts face challenges in dealing with too many buildings, whether due to a temporary dip in student population or a more permanent change in the community. Striking a balance between maintaining the facilities owned and operated by a district and meeting current student need is a daunting challenge.

Saturation is not a new challenge for school districts. Educating students is expensive, and districts have carefully built schools to match the number of students within their boundaries. Without precise planning, school district expenses would quickly spiral out of control. To avoid this, school districts have predetermined the precise number of educational and extracurricular offerings and choices they need to serve their students.

But saturation as a result of chartered schools has presented school districts with an obstacle they have never encountered. With chartered schools, districts are losing students at a rate they cannot predict. And as stated previously, fewer students mean decreased funding. Districts must make cuts to enable them to maintain their facilities and students. If parents take notice of the consequences of shrinking budgets, they will be motivated to enroll their children in competing chartered schools, and this will further decrease districts' funding.

Although colocation may seem a viable option for a district dealing with too many school buildings, as the educational establishment points out, the practice can negatively affect student learning. While a traditional public school's classrooms may be designated as vacant and therefore qualify as eligible for chartered school use, they may in fact be used for music and physical education classes, classroom material storage, and more. In addition, colocation can stretch thin a campus's facilities and resources, such as cafeterias, restrooms, libraries, computer labs, gyms, and custodial staff.

The different school cultures of chartered schools and traditional public schools sharing one campus can lead to conflicts as well. For example, a chartered school may require uniforms, while the traditional public school does not. Or the campuses may have conflicting bell and athletic schedules. Independence High School (IHS) in Santa Clara County, California, colocated with a magnet school and three chartered schools: ACE, Downtown College Prep, and KIPP. In 2015, IHS parents, community members, and staff circulated a petition citing their grievances, including concerns over campus safety, scheduling conflicts, parking congestion, and insufficient facilities. After collecting nearly three thousand signatures, they submitted their petition to the school board.

Another means for a school district to deal with excess buildings is to sell the property. This is often not the best long-term option, and when districts possess surplus property, they typically hold on to it and, if possible, lease it. As mentioned previously, school districts are reluctant to sell off surplus facilities because their student population may grow over time. In this instance, school districts calculate that maintaining an underused facility is cheaper over the long term than selling it off and having to purchase property in the future at a higher real estate cost.

Although districts are often highly criticized for hanging on to property, their rationale is often sound because redevelopment is common. If in ten years a district intends to buy back property or comparable property, doing so could be cost-prohibitive. Would leasing excess property to chartered schools be an action that supports both traditional and chartered school efforts?

Single-family homes today may be filled with older homeowners. In the future, apartments may replace these, and families with children may occupy them. Then, smaller apartments would be replaced by larger apartments that would bring more students into a school district. While a school district may not be able to fill a campus with students in the present, this may change in the future.

Educational Establishment Pushback

The monopoly school districts have on educating the students within its boundaries is essential for districts to develop accurate budgets and uphold the educational social contract.

To avoid saturation brought about by chartered schools, the educational establishment has sought to make it increasingly more difficult for chartered schools to set up shop. Stricter charter school laws create expensive and time-consuming roadblocks for those interested in establishing chartered schools. In some states where school districts are authorizers, chartered schools can open only within the district's boundaries.

In Louisiana, as noted by the Center for Education Reform, those engaging in pushback have continuously put forward laws that would restrict chartered school growth in a state that, in the wake of Hurricane Katrina, relied on chartered schools to educate tens of thousands of its students whose campuses were demolished by one of the worst natural disasters in US history. Some of the proposed laws sought to outright ban the authorization of new chartered schools.

In states that allow or mandate colocation on traditional public school facilities that have unused space, districts engaging in pushback have resisted disclosing their available facilities, thereby blocking chartered schools' legal rights.

School districts have also blocked colocation altogether, obstructing a chartered school's hopes to educate a community's student population. According to the *Los Angeles Times* on April 11, 2016, in a landmark court case, the Los Angeles Unified School District was found guilty of violating state law by failing to provide rent-free classroom space to Ivy Academia. The settlement required the district to pay $7.1 million to the San Fernando Valley–based chartered school.

Across the country, those opposed to chartered school growth are aggressively fighting to limit the entities designated to authorize chartered schools. The combination of onerous charter school law and limited authorizations results in ever-higher barriers for those seeking to open new chartered schools, thereby slowing their growth.

2. Strong Charter Law Allows Multiple Charter Authorizers

The Chartered School's Perspective

Effective charter school law gives its schools the autonomy that allows them to innovate, positively influence traditional public schools, and improve the lives of millions of students across the country. This autonomy and innovation will increase with the availability of multiple charter authorizers, which are entities that open these much-needed educational doors for prospective chartered schools.

While examples exist of chartered schools that have fallen short of the promise of educational reform, overly restrictive charter school laws unfairly punish schools that have delivered remarkable results and have developed breakthrough strategies that have improved educational outcomes and will continue to do so for years to come. The remarkable results of these exemplary schools have been, in large part, due to charter laws that encourage independence that leads to innovation.

For every example of a chartered school that has underperformed, there are multiple traditional public schools that have failed to deliver quality, lasting education to their students and communities. The educational establishment, time and time again, has refused to aggressively challenge and hold accountable the bureaucratic institutions and entrenched self-interests that allow the nation's most poorly performing traditional public schools to perpetuate their culture of failure.

In states where chartered schools have been allowed to thrive and grow, students have benefitted. In California, the California Charter Schools Association (CCSA) published a study in 2016 demonstrating that chartered schools in the Golden State send more students to the University of California (UC) and California State University (CSU) systems than do traditional public schools in the state. In particular, African American, Latino, and low-income students who attend chartered schools gain entry into the flagship UC system at nearly twice the rate of their traditional public school counterparts.

Given that, in proportion to their population in California, African American and Latino students are underrepresented in the UC and CSU systems, chartered schools are more effectively narrowing the achievement gap compared to traditional public schools. Based on these findings, as emphasized in the CCSA's *A Step Up*, a framework that encourages the growth of chartered schools means improved access for students who have historically struggled to gain a foothold in higher education.

More and multiple types of authorizers mean a higher number of students will benefit from the contributions chartered schools make to public education. In addition to school districts, statewide chartered school commissions, colleges, and universities can be chartered school authorizers. For example, in Arizona, state boards and universities have been assigned as authorizers. And in New York, the State University of New York is a higher-education authorizer. According to the Center for Education Reform, "states with multiple chartering authorities have almost three and a half times more charter schools than states that only allow local school board approval." By increasing the number of authorizers, the number of chartered schools will increase.

In an expanded authorizer setting, it is vital that authorizers have the staffing and resources necessary to provide effective oversight, and those chartered schools that are out of compliance with charter law should have their charters revoked. When authorizers fall short of their responsibilities, chartered school wrongdoing goes unpunished. This is unacceptable to both the educational establishment and the educational reform movement. If a chartered school is chronically underperforming, it should be closed. But then again, so should underperforming traditional public schools.

Widespread stories of chartered schools failing students have damaged the reputation of chartered schools across the country, particularly chartered schools that perform at or far above the level of traditional public schools. Biased mainstream media coverage frequently highlights poorly performing chartered schools while neglecting to report on the countless examples of traditional public school failures, but the truth is the chartered school movement has dramatically improved the public education system.

The chartered school movement has expanded options for parents and has given them a voice in a public education landscape that has for too long refused to hear their appeals for change and choice.

Authorizer quality is also important. Authorizers should have the resources necessary to do their job well, which includes fully understanding the mission of each chartered school they are charged with overseeing. In many states, however, authorizers have a high caseload of chartered schools, which reduces their ability to provide impeccable oversight.

In general, the educational reform movement is opposed to district authorizers. When the school district that views a chartered school within its boundaries as a competitor is also its authorizer, this presents a conflict of interest. At the same time, designating another entity, such as a university, as an authorizer seems like a simple solution. But universities often do not have the budget or staff to take on this large responsibility. The same is the case for states and counties. The reformers believe chartered schools and their students are best served with multiple charter authorizers. For example, independent commissions or community-based organizations could also sponsor or oversee chartered schools. There are many possibilities and creative opportunities in the development of a system that takes a broader view of entities qualified to authorize chartered schools.

The Educational Establishment's Perspective

The uptick in chartered schools as a result of more authorizers will result in saturation, which will hinder a district's ability to fulfill the educational social contract. To increase chartered school compliance and decrease saturation, the educational establishment seeks a charter law model that assigns fewer, not more, authorizers. This is because more authorizers would presuppose more chartered schools being approved, which the educational establishment does not want. A scenario where there are multiple avenues for charter approval lessens a school district's control, and the resulting growth of chartered schools could have a devastating effect on a school district.

Also, many examples of chartered school malfeasance point to authorizers that have neglected to provide thorough oversight of the schools under their watch. In general, this is a quality-versus-quantity issue. The quality of an authorizer's oversight decreases as the number of chartered schools he or she oversees increases.

When authorizers fail to fulfill their responsibilities, the likelihood of a chartered school violating charter law increases. The educational establishment undoubtedly contends that multiple authorizers will lead not only to more chartered schools but also to an increase in authorizers that do not adequately hold themselves accountable.

Educational Establishment Pushback

States that have resisted chartered school growth have done so precisely by limiting the entities that are designated as authorizers. For example, in Oregon and Virginia, school boards are the only authorizing entity, and in New Jersey, the state is the sole authorizer.

Those fighting educational reform are lobbying for laws that limit the number of entities that can be designated as authorizers. They also support charter law that curbs chartered school autonomy. Under this model, less is better: Fewer authorizers means more centralized governance, which means chartered schools would be subject to an increased number of strictly enforced regulations. In addition, fewer authorizers may slow the growth of chartered schools, thus preventing saturation, which limits a district's ability to establish accurate budgets necessary to educate its students. Traditional public schools that have neglected the needs of their communities and the students they are charged with teaching have ignored the voices of parents. They have consistently failed to uphold the educational social contract and continue to go unpunished.

3. Strong Charter Law Exempts Chartered Schools from Most Laws and Regulations Governing School Districts

The Chartered School's Perspective

Exemplary chartered schools should be given the independence they need to continue delivering outstanding results. Innovation and adaptability are two qualities of chartered schools. Their ability to leverage these two strengths is largely due to their independence. Chartered schools are able to meet the needs of the students by quickly adopting new strategies and targeting instruction to the specific needs of their student population. Traditional public schools are generally slow to adapt to change. This may be intentional: A school district's culture may be entrenched in tradition and an organizational culture that is cautious or downright skeptical of change. Or this may be unintentional: A school district may be eager to adopt a new program, but layers of regulation may serve as bureaucratic shackles.

For chartered schools to be at the forefront of breakthrough pedagogy, they must never be bound to the same compliance framework as traditional public schools. Doing so would alter their fundamental design. Rather than bring about rapid public education improvements, which have been their hallmark and legacy, they would become a slightly modified version of traditional public education—replete with the institutional shortcomings the educational establishment has failed to address for decades, as noted by the *Orange County Register*.

Those states that adopted charter school law early in the chartered school movement tend to have a compliance framework that is more flexible than that of states that adopted charter laws when the pushback movement grew in influence and power. These early adopter states designed their charter laws to encourage autonomy that would foster innovation. Less restrictive charter law is one reason states at the forefront of the chartered school movement—such as Arizona, California, Minnesota, and New York—have much higher numbers of chartered schools when compared to states with charter school laws that were established later.

Think of chartered schools as mini school districts that follow a different set of rules from traditional school districts. Unlike traditional public schools, which are not autonomous and must follow district policies, practices, and procedures, chartered schools have no district above them, and their compliance framework is separate from that of traditional school districts. This independence has resulted in breakthrough strategies and decision-making processes that encourage schools to adapt quickly to change.

If a chartered school determines its students require additional classroom time and instruction, it may extend instructional hours or even offer weekend classes. In many states, doing so would violate collective-bargaining agreements outlined in a traditional public school's compliance framework. In other words, the law would prohibit extending instructional hours. If chartered schools are required to abide by the same compliance framework as traditional public schools, they would lose the institutional strengths that, from the start, were designed to set them apart from traditional public schools.

The difference between a traditional school district's compliance framework and charter school laws is significant. For instance, traditional public schools must abide by strict rules regarding teaching materials. In the case of textbooks, school districts can purchase books only from a state-approved list. A district may believe a certain textbook will serve its students' needs best. But if it does not appear on the state-approved list, the district is barred from purchasing it.

In the case of charter law, most chartered schools are not bound to state-approved lists. If a chartered school finds a book that will serve the needs of its students more effectively than one that appears on a state-approved list, it is free to use it for instruction as long as it is compliant with the law. (For example, books cannot have a religious bias.) This is one example among many that point to the strengths of chartered school autonomy.

Control over their policies, practices, and procedures creates a learning environment that allows chartered schools to put teaching and learning first. Well-written charter law gives chartered schools the ability to implement student-centered curriculum, as well as policies, practices, and procedures that are not entrenched in a bureaucracy more focused on its own interests than those of students and parents.

Traditional school districts are forced to abide by a complex compliance framework. But this is no grounds to require chartered schools to comply with the same set of standards. In Ted Kolderie's *The Split Screen Strategy*, the author states, "Legislators intended chartering to introduce both innovation and accountability." Kolderie goes on to describe how, from their start, chartered schools were designed to be "independent entities on contract to districts or to the state or entities designated by the state." Thus, a separate compliance framework was not an afterthought in the design of chartered schools. Rather, it was a means to foster independence as part of its original blueprint. Requiring chartered schools to suddenly conform to a school district's compliance framework is anathema to the mission and objectives of chartered schools and to their founding principles.

While employee work conditions are typically covered in both the traditional public school compliance framework and charter school law, in general, the rules governing traditional public schools are more specific.

When it comes to accountability, the chartered school movement believes charter laws should strike a balance between protecting the best interests of students and providing thriving chartered schools the autonomy that has brought about high-quality results. The formula for successful chartered schools across the nation is working, parents are thrilled with the results, and students are achieving. This success is both a blessing and a curse. As high-performing chartered schools increase market share, school districts are losing revenue. Thus, the cycle of educational establishment pushback begins.

When it comes to trade unions, the employees within each chartered school should have the option to unionize or not unionize. In fact, one aspect of strong charter law is granting chartered schools the ability to join unions. Overall, while some chartered schools have elected to unionize, the vast majority have not.

For special education and English-language learner students, chartered schools have leveraged and will continue to leverage their innovative culture to develop strategies that meet the needs of today's diverse student population. The chartered school model is well suited to providing solutions to the greatest challenges public education faces today.

Chartered schools should be held to the highest levels of accountability, and charter law must allow schools to maintain the independence that is their hallmark. As Kolderie described, accountability is one of the building blocks of chartered schools. Therefore, contrary to mainstream media portrayals, educational reform leaders embrace rather than eschew accountability.

When chartered schools fail to uphold charter law, authorizers should revoke their charters. This accountability measure has no equivalent in the traditional public school framework. Consistently underperforming traditional public schools rarely, if ever, are forced to improve or close shop.

The Educational Establishment's Perspective

In general, the educational establishment believes charter law allows chartered schools to operate with less transparency and accountability when compared to traditional public schools.

The accountability mechanisms set in place to oversee chartered schools have not kept pace with their growth. Too many examples of chartered schools behaving badly mean that chartered schools need more laws and regulations, not fewer. To compete in a fair public education environment, both chartered schools and traditional schools should follow the same or similar rules and regulations.

Currently, charter law varies from state to state, and the laws can be dramatically different. Under this patchwork of state regulation, measuring chartered school performance on a national scale is nearly impossible, and chartered schools receive minimal levels of oversight unheard of in traditional public education. In the case of traditional public schools, each state's compliance framework is different, but all share many aspects in common. They are all highly detailed documents. Overall, the compliance framework chartered schools must follow is less specific and rigid than that of traditional public schools.

Indeed, school districts must observe an astonishingly long list of policies, practices, and procedures that dictate all aspects of how they are run. As traditional public schools have grown, so have their policies, practices, and procedures. The California Education Code (usually called Ed Code) is more than twenty-two hundred pages and divided into sixty-nine parts, with as many as twelve subparts per section. Deciphering the massive document requires legal expertise, and its contents are constantly revised. From school bus emissions to education in state prison, if you have a question about traditional public education in California, you will find it in the Ed Code. The Golden State's original charter law was a mere fourteen pages. Even at its current length of over two hundred pages, it pales in comparison to California's Ed Code.

The compliance framework traditional public schools must abide by requires evaluating the quality of a district's program. Schools are assessed on student performance, graduation rates, teacher retention, and student discipline. Much of this information is public record. In addition, school board meeting minutes are made public. The multiple transparency mandates engender high levels of public accountability. Depending on the state, its charter law may or may not have such assessment and reporting requirements, including stipulations to publicly publish board of directors meetings (this is the chartered school equivalent of school board meetings because chartered schools do not have publicly elected school boards). Chartered school board of directors meetings are usually not required to occur with any set frequency. School districts, however, must have district board meetings at least once per month.

Educational Establishment Pushback

Those engaging in pushback argue that the very charter school laws that allow for flexibility and autonomy give those schools an unfair advantage. Even if a school district wanted to apply a certain breakthrough methodology, policy, practice, or procedure, if it conflicted with its compliance framework, it would be prohibited from doing so. In contrast, a chartered school may be able to institute the same program while remaining in compliance with a state's more flexible charter school law. But the chartered schools' compliance framework that allows its schools to be more innovative should not justify changing the rules for traditional public schools that have improved the lives of millions of students.

As a method of pushback, public education proponents are advocating chartered schools' authorizers to oversee and measure chartered school performance using the same standards on which traditional schools are evaluated. In other words, both should have to follow the same compliance framework. Doing so will reduce instances of chartered schools failing to act in students' best interests because they will be held to the same high transparency and accountability standards as traditional public schools. In fact, those behind pushback believe charter school laws themselves are largely to blame for chartered schools that fall short of expectations.

Rather than pushback, the educational establishment should embrace the improvements successful chartered schools have developed and determine how to bring about the changes necessary to replicate these innovations within their schools.

4. Strong Charter Law Provides Chartered Schools with Fiscal Flexibility

The Chartered School's Perspective

The chartered school model takes a businesslike approach to budgeting. It is revenue neutral, relies on a balanced budget and good business practices, and accommodates flexibility, the uniqueness of a learning community, and long-range strategic planning.

The strategic-planning component means a budget can focus on the long term, which includes addressing entrepreneurial and creative opportunities for investment into the organization. In the case of traditional public education, its budgeting guidelines require school districts to spend the money they receive every year. The way in which they spend their money is highly regulated as well. This prevents school districts from effectively planning for the long term.

The traditional public education business process focuses on the federal, state, and local governments controlling budgeting. This top-down model is inherently paternalistic. It is as if the government oversight bodies are telling school districts, "We don't trust you, so we'll make rigid rules that engender sameness for all school districts."

In the chartered school model, each organization is in control of its budgeting process. The corporate model is bottom-up. This arrangement requires legal compliance and following standard accounting practices. It entrusts each chartered school to develop a process that puts students' needs first and allows schools to put together the best educational program possible. Funds can be spent toward growing a school and long-term plans that may require years of steady investment according to a school's strategic plan.

Chartered school fiscal flexibility is more similar to the corporate approach to budgeting than it is to the traditional public education budgeting model. This makes sense because chartered schools are small corporations that are intended to function in a market-driven public education landscape.

While the traditional public school's fiscal accountability model is intended to engender ethical practices and avoid malfeasance, it can also prevent schools from acting in their best interests. The chartered school model gives schools the ability to customize their budgetary process to accommodate their particular needs. Many traditional school leaders envy this inherent flexibility.

Both traditional public school and chartered school budgets must follow the budget guidelines in their respective compliance framework. Most chartered schools operate under the corporate law formula. This allows chartered schools' budgets to follow principles driven by programs that result in positive student outcomes. Chartered schools' budgetary guidelines allow them to take a pragmatic approach to education: When a chartered school identifies a need, it can act quickly to fill it. Rather than be restricted by one-size-fits-all line-item budget guidelines that are part of a district's compliance framework, chartered schools are able to implement custom strategies to address their greatest challenges and develop successful programs. The fact that corporate law gives chartered schools freedom not afforded to school districts means exactly that—chartered schools are not bound to traditional public school's line-item budgets.

Under most current charter school law, intermediaries, such as counties and chartered school commissions, receive state funds designated for chartered schools and are responsible for distributing them. When counties or chartered school commissions are responsible for funding chartered schools, they add layers of rules and regulations that restrict chartered school autonomy. This is one reason chartered schools favor direct funding.

WHAT IS DIRECT FUNDING?

When counties or chartered school commissions are responsible for funding chartered schools, each layer of administration takes a percentage of what it receives from the state to cover overhead costs, in addition to filtering its decisions through an added level of rules and regulations at each step.

In a direct-funding model, chartered schools receive funding directly from the state, thereby avoiding intermediaries. Under this arrangement, chartered schools are better able to negotiate the rules and regulations authorizers place on them in a way that protects their best interests. Direct funding increases chartered school autonomy.

Fiscal autonomy allows chartered schools to operate more efficiently than their district counterparts. Many times, chartered schools are not required to follow traditional school rules regarding bidding, purchasing, and acquiring facilities. They have more flexibility to create, experiment, and innovate. Autonomy gives chartered schools the ability to make personnel, instructional, and facilities decisions that are able to quickly meet the needs of the populations they serve.

If a chartered school sought to purchase a new facility, most charter law places no budgetary restrictions on the school's plans to save money toward its expansion efforts. In this regard, they function similarly to mini school districts, and under charter law, they are able to make their own decisions. Through prudent planning, some chartered schools have amassed reserves large enough to meet the objectives of their strategic plans. For example, if purchasing a facility is part of a strategic plan, then accumulating enough funds to buy it in cash can result in negotiating a more favorable purchase price, as well as long-term savings, versus seeking financing and paying interest. Furthermore, owning property increases a chartered school's credibility and sustainability.

Within traditional education, most school-site principals are never part of the acquisition and sale of district real estate holdings. Chartered school leaders often have a more sophisticated vision of the tremendous requirements of running a successful program.

While both traditional schools and chartered schools usually must submit their budgets for approval following rigorous county procedures, corporate law allows significant flexibility in regard to how chartered schools spend their money. Rather than having to comply with line-item budgets, corporate law allows chartered schools to determine how much money they will allocate toward personnel, instructional materials, facilities, and other expenses. Thus, instead of following one-size-fits-all budget guidelines, corporate law grants chartered schools flexibility with how they spend and save.

If a chartered school sees a need to develop an advertising and marketing budget, it is able to create a line item to account for this expense. Traditional districts rarely have such a need, since they rely on their long-standing public education monopoly to attract students to their campuses. Even if a traditional district sees a need to invest in advertising and marketing, if no such line exists in its budget or if it is seriously underfunded, the district may be limited in its capacity to promote its schools. With the onset of chartered schools, many of which have robust advertising and marketing campaigns, traditional public schools have realized they are confronting a market-driven force that is reducing their main revenue source—the students—who are leaving their classrooms and flocking to chartered schools.

As far as executive compensation is concerned, because chartered schools operate following a corporate model, leaders are paid in line with corporate standards. This allows chartered schools to maintain competitive hiring practices to retain the most qualified individuals to lead their organizations. Many of these leaders have brought about innovations and improvements informed by perspectives outside the educational establishment. These chartered leaders perform at will and must demonstrate success in meeting their organization's strategic plans.

The Educational Establishment's Perspective

When it comes to income and expenses, school districts must abide by strict line-item budget guidelines that appear in their compliance framework. These rules outline how purchases are accounted for and where money is spent. If an item does not appear as a line in the budget, the district cannot save or spend money toward it. Districts also must follow prohibitive reserve guidelines that limit their ability to save income from year to year. This prevents school districts from investing in their infrastructure, including building new facilities.

Furthermore, only county offices and school districts can purchase property. Individual school sites within a district cannot because they are not autonomous entities.

The educational establishment argues that fiscal autonomy is problematic because it leads to less financial transparency. Traditional school district budgets must maintain higher levels of public disclosure when compared to chartered school budgets. Lower transparency leads to lower accountability, and lower accountability may result in intentional or unintentional fiscal errors.

The publicly elected boards of traditional public schools add a level of accountability to the budget process. These individuals oversee and approve how districts spend their resources. They are held accountable for the strengths and weaknesses of a budget. Poor decision-making on the part of administrators or elected officials can result in their being fired or losing elections. Under charter law, boards of directors and trustees oversee and approve budgets. Unlike school board members, they are not publicly elected officials and can be hired and fired without a public election.

Within a district's compliance framework, all records are public, and they must be free and accessible. Rules regarding right of access mean anyone can petition a school district to disclose the salaries of its employees, including superintendents. The corporate law under which chartered schools operate requires varying degrees of access depending on the charter laws where a chartered school operates.

At the same time, the law mandates that both traditional public schools and chartered schools submit budgets to county departments of education. In addition, chartered schools have to also provide budgets to authorizing agencies when applicable.

In the end, both traditional and chartered schools are held fiscally accountable. They must remain transparent and formally submit budget documents to districts, counties, states, and chartered school commissions.

Educational Establishment Pushback

Those engaging in pushback believe the corporate law standard under which chartered schools operate allows chartered schools spending and saving flexibility not afforded to traditional public schools. This creates an unfair competitive advantage for chartered schools.

Pushback aims not only to hold both traditional public schools and chartered schools to the same budget guidelines but also to subject public monies chartered schools receive to the same levels of educational code restrictions as traditional public schools. More regulation would give external oversight bodies, such as authorizers, increased authority over the personnel, instructional, and facilities decisions chartered schools make. Installing multiple layers of administration that manage chartered school funding and compliance increases accountability. Thus, the educational establishment believes counties and authorizers should all play an important role in chartered school oversight. What pushback neglects to address, however, are the multiple examples of the misappropriation of funds within the traditional public education system. In a high-profile case, Michelle Rhee, shortly after being appointed chancellor of the District of Columbia Public Schools, invited the media to witness the fiscal waste she discovered within the school district she was charged to lead.

In front of TV cameras, Rhee pointed out multiple pallets of textbooks and school supplies collecting dust in district warehouses. These resources were never used, were stored indefinitely, and demonstrated the fiscal irresponsibility of those within the school district charged with overseeing taxpayer dollars and the learning materials students required. Thus, despite the so-called transparent practices school districts are required to follow, there is no shortage of financial mismanagement examples and unethical fiscal practices.

5. Strong Charter Law Stipulates Full Funding for Chartered Schools

The Chartered School's Perspective

Full funding means equitable funding. Whatever amount traditional public schools receive, chartered schools are entitled to the same amount—no exception. This includes funding for transportation and per-pupil funding, regardless of a chartered school's transportation needs or its mode of instructional delivery, which includes online, blended, and independent study, or flexible instruction.

According to a 2014 report published by the Center for Education Reform, chartered schools are funded an average of 36 percent less than traditional public schools. This amounts to an average of $7,131 per pupil per year for chartered schools versus $11,184 per pupil per year for traditional schools. Chartered schools spend on average $7,568 per pupil, which means they must generate $437 more per pupil per year than they actually receive in funding.

Chartered schools are public schools and are entitled to the same funding as traditional schools. Chartered school students deserve the same rights as traditional school students. Under local-control funding formulas, funding belongs to students, not school districts.

Chartered schools uphold the paradigm of "where the student goes, money and control should follow." This standard is based on the premise that chartered schools are entitled to full funding without exception. The amount of money states allocate to each student should follow the student, no matter where he or she attends school. In other words, the average daily attendance amount for each student is attached to the student, not the school site. Chartered schools and traditional schools are the custodians of this money, not the arbiters of how much each should receive.

When traditional school districts challenge the "where the student goes, money and control should follow" model, they are advocating for a two-class funding hierarchy where traditional schools are at the top and chartered schools and their students are second-class citizens residing underneath. This hierarchy is both unfair and harmful to public education and, most importantly, to the students schools are charged with educating.

According to the Center for Education Reform's "Survey of America's Charter Schools 2014," most chartered schools are not compensated for the cost of securing and maintaining their facilities. Thus, most chartered schools must find revenue sources outside average daily attendance to cover expenses associated with renting or purchasing facilities, as well as maintaining them. Under these fiscally austere circumstances, those at the forefront of educational reform may have limited options. They may have to open their chartered schools in retail spaces, office buildings, or vacant and neglected public school facilities. This is certainly not the case for traditional public schools, whose districts receive funding for facilities and their maintenance. Despite these adverse circumstances, chartered schools have managed to rise above the challenges they face, put students' needs first, and develop industry-leading outcomes.

Imagine the untapped potential chartered schools would unleash if they were given a full-funding fiscal landscape to till.

The Educational Establishment's Perspective

While many associate traditional public schools with classrooms and teachers, maintaining extracurricular programs can equal the resources required to maintain classrooms and employ teachers. In fact, many large high school campuses rival the size and resources of colleges. You will find football fields, auditoriums, film studios, aquatic facilities, large parking structures, and more. Students participate in athletics, drama, band, and field trips. High schools with robust extracurricular (also called cocurricular) programs may spend 40–50 percent of their budgets supporting and maintaining these facilities and programs. The bottom line is that maintaining school facilities and programs is expensive.

From their outset, chartered schools were established to focus on teaching and learning. Their campuses may be on traditional public school facilities, in strip malls, in warehouses, online, or in a combination of the preceding. This means the cost to operate a chartered school varies widely. Chartered schools without cocurricular programs do not require the same amount of funding as a traditional public school that must maintain costly facilities and programs.

The funding models for chartered schools and traditional public schools should reflect the differences each has in its operational costs. If a traditional public school's programs and facilities cost more to operate than those of a chartered school, then the traditional public schools should receive more per-student funding than their chartered school counterparts with less expensive overhead.

When it comes to how schools are funded, the rules vary from state to state. In general, county departments of education approve school budgets and submit them to the state. Once the state reviews and approves what the county department of education has submitted, the state sends quarterly checks to the county. The county then takes a portion of the funding it received from the state to pay for overhead costs and sends money to the school district.

In most instances, chartered schools receive their state funding from the county level or approved authorizer. At each stage of the funding process, the receiver will take a percentage of the proceeds to cover the administrative costs before sending funds to the next level. In addition, the receiving entity of funds applies rules to the chartered school regarding how the school can spend the money it receives. These layers of oversight hold chartered schools more accountable for the money they receive. In most areas, the educational establishment would like all chartered school funding to be sent to the school district. From the school district, the funds would be sent to the chartered school, as opposed to the current practice, which is funding from the state directly to the chartered school.

Educational Establishment Pushback

Chartered schools should be funded based on their needs. If a non-site-based chartered school requires less money to operate than a traditional public school, that chartered school should receive less funding. If a designated fund for a traditional school does not exist for a chartered school, the chartered school should not receive that money. For instance, say a traditional public school has an account line for transportation, and a chartered school does not provide transportation. The account lines for that traditional public school and that chartered school would not be the same. In addition, chartered schools should be held to the same budget principles as traditional public schools.

The educational establishment takes a custodial approach to the students and the money and control attached to them. It believes it is entitled to all public school funding that students within its boundaries receive. The underlying mind-set is one of scarcity rather than abundance: Any money a school district gives to chartered schools is depleting its rightful funds. This was not always the case. Early in chartered school history, many school districts and chartered schools worked in a spirit of collaboration. Districts provided chartered schools important services, including professional development, instructional guidance, and budget analysis. As chartered schools grew and posed a threat to traditional schools, districts viewed chartered schools as a financial burden and either withheld services or charged for those rendered.

In the eyes of the educational establishment, control is what is at stake. As chartered schools grow, so does their political and legislative capital. When chartered schools have more control over funding, they will have the fiscal resources they need to fuel an educational reform engine with boundless potential. The educational reform movement has within itself the ability to improve student outcomes in a way unseen in the history of public education.

The educational establishment has both witnessed what chartered schools are capable of achieving and recognized the educational reform movement has just begun tapping into its seemingly limitless potential. The educational establishment claims its oversight is necessary to hold chartered schools fiscally accountable. But behind the altruistic auspices is its true motive: control. By maintaining control over funding, the educational establishment maintains its institutional monopoly for delivering public education. Pushback is a means of maintaining control and starving the growth of the educational reform movement. Controlling funding forms an essential weapon in the educational establishment's pushback arsenal.

When Traditional Public Schools and Chartered Schools Work Together, All Students Benefit

Strong charter law is based on putting students' needs first. It allows for an unrestricted number of chartered schools, as well as students that can attend them; they allow multiple charter authorizers; and they exempt chartered schools from most laws and regulations governing school districts.

Rather than concentrating resources and time into pushback, the educational establishment would gain from working with chartered schools to improve outcomes for the students they are ostensibly charged with serving. In fact, many school districts across the nation are experiencing an existential crisis. By adopting the breakthrough and sound practices chartered schools have developed, these districts will improve their chances of averting disaster.

In the end, pushback is costly, is stressful, and most importantly, does little to improve student outcomes. Waging war and facing a battle of apocalyptic proportions is not predetermined. By putting the needs of students first and laying self-interest aside, both traditional public schools and chartered schools win.

Chapter 6

OBSERVATIONS

THE ANNUAL CALIFORNIA Charter School Conference, sponsored by the California Charter School Association, is similar to other yearly gatherings for large membership organizations. Men and women come from all over the Golden State to attend the event. Attendees, lodged in nearby hotels, participate in plenary and breakout sessions. Thousands of people travel from near and far to experience renewal, growth, and camaraderie.

All participants share a common passion: education reform. With their new vision of public education, each man and woman attending the event strives to improve the lives of students. The event invites a who's who of the chartered school movement to give dynamic keynote speeches to packed auditoriums. CEOs, authors, teachers, administrators, and consultants host a dizzying list of workshops that address the movement's most pressing interests. They explore a wide variety of topics, including legal compliance, advocacy, management, assessment, curriculum, instruction, and site operations. Over the course of five days, attendees have countless opportunities to meet one another and strengthen their networks of passionate educators.

Every day within their local chartered schools, teachers and administrators must meet the needs of the students and parents they serve. The day-to-day duties of running a first-class educational program are both immense and demanding. Under these high-pressure site-level conditions, it is easy to lose sight of the amazing work that takes place in chartered schools located in other cities and counties across the nation.

Annual conferences, such as the CCSA event, provide essential professional development. They remind all attendants that the chartered school movement consists of a vibrant community of like-minded individuals. All participants share in the promise of educational reform. In this way, the CCSA conference represents a blend of the *extraordinary* and the *ordinary*, a testament to everyone's daily hard work melding with the magic of growing a cutting-edge system.

First, the extraordinary: From the start, those within the chartered school movement have revolutionized public schools unlike any other educational reform movement before it. Annual conferences are not only a celebration; they are also a merging of minds with the goal of continually improving the chartered school model.

Second, the ordinary: Like all large and established organizations, the impeccably organized and highly attended annual CCSA event demonstrates the legitimacy, strength, and impact of the chartered school movement. In fact, 2018 marks the twenty-fifth anniversary of the conference.

The CCSA convention is just one example among many of well-orchestrated gatherings across the country of chartered school teachers, administrators, leaders, and parents. Events such as these demonstrate that, far from fringe or fad, chartered schools are just as permanent and enduring in the future of public education as their traditional public school counterparts.

Without a doubt, chartered schools are here to stay. But unlike other established organizations that succumb to comfort and complacency, those at the forefront of the chartered school movement are steadfast in their commitment to continually improving the breakthrough educational model. Innovation, combined with a dedication to incorporating new, promising pedagogy, is at the heart of what makes chartered schools a force that has forever changed public education for the better.

As an expression of the educational reform movement's unwavering dedication to improvement and continual self-reflection, in this chapter, we will perform a SWOT analysis. SWOT stands for strengths, weaknesses, opportunities, and threats. It is an assessment tool frequently performed in the corporate world. This chapter's SWOT focus exemplifies the chartered school movement's dedication to implementing successful strategies that come from competitive, successful corporate models. This SWOT analysis of the educational reform movement will provide insight into where chartered schools stand today and the direction they are headed tomorrow.

STRENGTH: Chartered Schools Are Here to Stay

The founding leaders of the chartered school movement were public education mavericks. Similar to all influential trailblazers, they had no prior paradigm to rely on, plenty of reason to succumb to fear of the unknown, an insatiable drive to create something out of nothing, and a dogged determination to move forward, no matter what setbacks stood in their way.

Driven by the entrepreneurial vision of America's culture of innovation, they were risk takers who sought to create safe and welcoming learning environments that leveraged breakthrough strategies. Little did these public education pioneers foresee that their idea would mushroom into a mainstream movement that has disrupted public education more than any other entity preceding it.

From a start-up cottage industry, chartered schools have grown in size and influence and, in some parts of the country, have even eclipsed the market share of traditional public schools. Today, students graduating from chartered schools and traditional public schools are viewed as equals in the eyes of college and university admissions departments.

WEAKNESS: Most Chartered Schools Are Operating on a Subsistence Level

Critical and biased media portrayals would have you thinking chartered schools are riding on waves of cash thanks to the largesse of billionaire philanthropists. According to these accounts, traditional public schools across the country are eking by on tax dollars coming from fiscally strapped government coffers. The urban myth of well-funded chartered schools belies the reality that the majority of chartered schools across the country are perpetually walking a financial tightrope without a safety net below to provide protection during fiscally lean years. The expectation of all schools is to maintain revenue-neutral budgets. Schools that neglect to have balanced budgets should rightfully be criticized for lacking sustainability.

Maintaining payroll obligations, meeting student needs, and on average, receiving less public funding compared to traditional public schools place relentless pressure on chartered schools. Most traditional schools have a large central district office they depend on. The district office is designed to deliver certain services to its schools and to fiscally support them based on a formula that ensures fair and equitable funding for each campus. This formula is commonly based on the number of students being served. Despite the multiple hurdles they face related to establishing and sustaining a successful educational program, chartered schools have courageously overcome obstacles and continued to thrive and grow.

Unfortunately, the more chartered schools succeed, the more the educational establishment perceives them as a threat and bolsters its pushback apparatus. New legislation, backed by the establishment, aims to strip chartered schools of the autonomy that is their hallmark. An oppressive regulatory environment weighs them down and runs contrary to their original mission. Chartered schools are charged with tiptoeing around multiple layers of red tape, which affects their ability to focus on meeting their students' greatest needs. For example, in Illinois, a state representative presented a bill in 2017 that would prohibit new charter campuses from opening within school districts with the state's lowest financial ratings, thereby adding a legislative hurdle that would slow if not stop chartered school growth in certain areas.

Human capital, time, and fiscal resources—in short supply for the vast majority of chartered schools—are spent racing around satisfying the latest regulatory hurdle, policy, or practice. Overregulation restricts chartered schools from fulfilling their innovative vision. Bloated bureaucracy slows or downright stops chartered schools from being able to scale up operations. This prevents them from educating even more children using successful strategies they and other members of the reform community have developed. The educational establishment is all too pleased with the unintended consequences of measures it justifies as increasing chartered school accountability. In other words, pushback is equal parts covert and overt.

In addition to educational establishment pushback, chartered schools face adjusting to rapid societal and pedagogical shifts. New curricular regulations and advances in mental health education, awareness related to bullying, transgender accommodations, and more are no doubt valuable. At the same time, they are significant items to add to chartered schools' already formidable to-do lists, especially if a school is struggling to provide cutting-edge, student-minded education on its threadbare budget.

OPPORTUNITY: The Public at Large Is Growing Increasingly Dissatisfied with the Educational Establishment

According to the forty-seventh annual poll co-published in 2015 by Phi Delta Kappan (PDK) International and Gallup, "Nearly two-thirds of Americans believe that 50% or fewer public school students in this country are receiving a high-quality education." In other words, according to public perception, generally speaking, traditional public education is not meeting the needs of the majority of students it is designated to teach. Although parents living in suburban areas consistently rank their neighborhood schools highly, based on our research, parents living in urban and socioeconomically disadvantaged areas were desperate for better-quality schools than what their local districts offered.

Our cross-country research confirmed many of the other PDK/Gallup poll findings. We observed that most parents of students living in socioeconomically disadvantaged urban communities and city centers with large ethnic minority populations consistently expressed dissatisfaction with their local traditional public schools. We did not intentionally seek out dissatisfied community members. In fact, we embarked on our investigation with an objective perspective prepared to observe and research without bias. But after meeting with community members and those within the educational establishment during our city visitations, we quickly discovered that, on an undeniably consistent basis, parents were desperately seeking better public school options beyond what their local school districts were offering.

According to our evaluation of *U.S. News & World Report*'s Best High Schools national rankings, which is based on data compiled on more than twenty-one thousand public high schools in fifty states and the District of Columbia, the country's top public high schools were mostly located in middle- to upper-class neighborhoods. Some of these communities were predominately white, while others were ethnically diverse. Whatever the ethnic makeup of the area, they all shared a similarly high socioeconomic status.

We spoke with Derrick Mitchell, who at the time was principal of Normandy High School in St. Louis, Missouri. At his high school, comprising an African American majority student body, the principal identified the low reading level of many of the school's students as Normandy High's greatest challenge. According to Mitchell, poverty has a far bigger negative impact on student performance than race does.

Comprehensively exploring the unequivocal and important relationship between a community's socioeconomic status and the general quality of its traditional public schools is beyond the scope of this book. With that said, through our investigation, we were inspired by educational reformers across the country taking on the challenges facing public schools located in struggling urban areas. For decades, these regions have been steeped in violence, neglect, poverty, and despair. In most cases, chartered schools in socioeconomically disadvantaged neighborhoods throughout the nation are providing a high-quality public education option to parents who have for too long been ignored by the educational establishment.

Through their chartered schools, these parents have been given a voice that has proven strong and unwavering in its demand for better public schools. Their voice is essential to the continued improvement of the education students receive, regardless of their socioeconomic status. Their demands for quality will not be ignored. Unless the educational establishment addresses the needs of parents empowered by options they previously did not have, it will continue to lose students to chartered schools. With the onset of chartered schools, parents know what safe, welcoming, and inspiring learning communities look like, and they will refuse to settle for anything that does not meet the new benchmark chartered schools have set for them.

Within public education circles, a common refrain is "for every academic year a student falls behind, it takes about four years for that student to catch up." Although one can argue about the exact amount of time a student who has fallen below grade level needs, no one will dispute that the effort and resources necessary for academically at-risk students to meet grade-level standards are immense.

Despite these obstacles, which often seem insurmountable, chartered schools across the country are taking the challenge head-on. Rather than give up on students whose academic performance is, at least in part, a result of a failed public education system, these schools and their staff are courageously dedicating themselves to providing students the support they need. They are creating vibrant learning cultures that have reengaged and encouraged students who have been neglected by poorly performing public schools—and parents have taken notice. When they see their children, whose previous attitudes about school ranged from indifferent to hostile, suddenly demonstrate enthusiasm and excitement about learning, mothers and fathers experience a relief and peace of mind that seemed otherwise unattainable.

Chartered schools are providing students, underserved by their local traditional public schools, a place where they can dare to dream and dare to learn.

In fact, in socioeconomically distressed neighborhoods, parents' demand to enroll their children in chartered schools frequently exceeds the capacity of these campuses. Critics of chartered schools argue that reports of waiting lists are inaccurate. They point out instances where student names have been duplicated on lists and lists have been out of date. While overreporting may occur, in our interviews we consistently met parents who confirmed the existence of waiting lists. They described their hopes in earnest to receive the call from the chartered schools informing them their child had made it off the waiting list and into the classroom, whether by specific admission or by random lottery. Within a short time frame, chartered schools have provided hope and inspiration to communities with otherwise limited options.

Many parents see chartered schools as an oasis in an otherwise arid public education landscape, one where districts have the facilities and funding but lack the vitality and ambition to inspire the students attending their schools. Some of these campuses have dashed the hopes and expectations of the parents and students they were designated by law to serve. They have been afflicted by the malaise of custodial neglect. This describes a condition where schools consistently meet only minimum regulatory requirements. It is custodial because these campuses provide what they are obligated to under the law—no more, no less. Thus, schools maintain compliance standards and an equitable learning environment. But custodial neglect indicates an omission of the exhaustive work necessary to create schools that engage and inspire their students.

In addition, custodial neglect typically means districts do not hold their campuses to the same rigorous performance standards of schools located in more affluent communities. Acting "above and beyond" and "exceeding expectations" are outside the lexicon of these low-achieving schools. Beyond minimum performance thresholds, parents must take it on themselves to have their children perform to the highest standards possible.

In the end, custodial neglect means students are provided merely what they need to succeed. From there, it is up to them to take or leave the resources they are offered. Custodial neglect is endemic in economically distressed regions, which are often also in our most densely populated urban areas. Thus, afflicted geographic regions serve the highest number of students.

High-stakes standardized testing and the public posting of letter grades for districts or schools have been efforts to address custodial neglect. These are examples of the educational establishment's attempts to push districts and their schools to improve student outcomes. But, as a result of bureaucracy and a general reliance on tradition, change within traditional public schools notoriously moves at a snail's pace. Initiatives to compel districts to improve student performance are a work in progress.

Chartered schools in urban centers throughout the United States have given parents options and outcomes that have historically been out of their reach. They have consistently succeeded in their mission to educate diverse populations. Parents representing underserved socioeconomic groups are voting with their feet and seeking chartered schools that meet the academic, safety, and emotional needs of their sons and daughters.

OPPORTUNITY: Chartered Schools Have Become a Disruptive Force within Public Schools

The more successful chartered schools become, they more they will be exposed to pushback. Or stated another way, the more traditional public schools lose revenue as a result of decreased market share, the more aggressively they will work to slow, if not stop, chartered school growth.

Traditional public schools are in a difficult place when they receive less state and federal funding. Parents demand the same levels of service year after year, regardless of shrinking budgets. And, with a diminished bottom line, districts are limited in their ability to invest and implement strategies designed to improve student outcomes. Thus, they look to bring revenue back by impeding or eliminating chartered schools in their district.

Pushback manifests in multiple forms. Common examples include onerous state and federal regulations related to instructional guidelines, funding requirements, governance, facilities, and operations. Adding compliance red tape restricts chartered schools' autonomy and creates higher barriers for entry for new chartered schools. As you learned previously, pushback is well funded, highly organized, and relentless.

The aim of pushback is to cast a cloud of regulatory confusion over chartered schools. The more chaos pushback creates within chartered schools, the more the educational establishment maintains its monopoly over public education. From a budgeting and staffing perspective, chartered schools are already spread thinly. They must reallocate their limited resources that could otherwise directly meet students' needs. Time and money, always in short supply, are spent chasing a dizzying series of ever-changing state and federal regulations. Remaining compliant is vital for a chartered school to stay open for business. But pleasing bureaucrats does not necessarily serve the interests of students and parents.

For the chartered schools that can remain viable despite this onslaught, pushback will only increase. As chartered schools continue to draw market share from districts, the mission and purpose of those at the front line of educational reform will grow. The good news is if the past is prologue, chartered schools will not succumb to the educational establishment's pushback fueled by the self-serving agendas of special interests. Educational reformers will continue to valiantly advocate on behalf of the communities they are called to serve.

OPPORTUNITY: The Concept of Being Market-Driven Has Found a Home within the K-12 Chartered School Culture

In a purely market-driven public education landscape, where parents would have multiple enrollment options for their children, traditional public schools across the nation would find themselves in deep trouble. If it were not for the monopoly they hold on public education, many school districts would fall into a fiscal crisis that could push them into insolvency.

This fear is at the heart of pushback. The educational establishment is an industry backed by billions of dollars, powerful special interest groups, and the public education brand, which represents one of the nation's most widely recognized and sacrosanct institutions. As you have learned throughout this book, chartered schools are public schools. But the educational establishment feeds public misconception and fears that chartered schools are dismantling public education. If presented as an "us versus them" face-off between chartered and traditional schools, then chartered schools are intent on taking away *our* public education.

Unfortunately, and over time, self-preservation has pushed school districts away from meeting students' needs and toward preserving the interests of each entity the educational establishment represents. The millions of individuals behind the educational establishment interpret the emergence of chartered schools as a threat to their fiscal and professional security. A market-driven approach has been a breakthrough model that has improved the lives of children across the country. Students, previously underserved by their traditional public schools, have access to quality education their parents had once only dreamed of. But rather than embrace chartered schools, the educational establishment views them as a rebuke of the status quo.

No one enjoys criticism. From first dates to first job interviews, fear of rejection from other people is at the core of the human condition. Similarly, those represented by the educational establishment are steadfast in their commitment to their model of public education, choosing to disregard signs that others in society feel they have gone off course. Many, for their entire lives, have existed within the public education ecosystem: They have attended K–12 public schools, graduated from public universities, received their teaching or administrative credentials from public institutions, and spent their careers as public school teachers or administrators. Many of these individuals view the educational reform movement's market-driven mission as a scathing critique of the paradigm in which they have invested their entire careers. According to this flawed perspective, accepting, let alone embracing, the chartered school approach would be anathema—an admission of traditional public education's fallibility, weaknesses, and downright failures.

All those dedicated members of the educational reform movement must continue the tireless work of informing the public of the mission and successes of chartered schools, dispelling false information intended to harm, and strengthening ties with the educational establishment whenever possible. Rather than a threat to public education to be stopped at all costs, educational reformers are visionaries and pioneers that fully embrace the promise of public education. Those at the forefront of this movement recognize that cutting-edge strategies are necessary to effectively educate a rapidly changing society. A market-driven model is a logical progression that aligns with the values of other major industries in our country, all bent on providing the highest-quality products and services.

OPPORTUNITY: Large Charter Management Organizations Were Not Part of Chartered Schools' Original Design

Chartered schools were first conceived as public schools with unparalleled levels of autonomy and flexibility that would encourage innovation for all schools. In the beginning, a spirit of collaboration and camaraderie rooted in a common purpose motivated the movement's early adopters. Stouthearted entrepreneurs saw an opportunity to grow a revolutionary model of public education ripe with potential.

Chartered schools soon found themselves growing faster than even the movement's founding leaders had envisioned. Today, they are competing head-to-head with traditional public schools. Back then, however, competition and taking market share were not part of chartered schools' original design. No one would have anticipated the rise of charter management organizations (CMOs) and the immense power and influence they would wield.

THE BIRTH OF CMOs

From the mid-1990s to the mid-2000s, chartered schools shifted from cottage industry to big business. This was in large part thanks to philanthropic financial support fueling the educational reform movement's ambitious growth and expansion efforts. During this time of rapid change within the educational reform movement, a new public education model emerged. Collectives of chartered schools, under one nonprofit corporate parent, began forming CMOs.

Prior to CMOs, the chartered schools scattered throughout a community acted independently of one another. With this new model, chartered schools would leverage the benefits of economies of scale and mirror similarly structured organizations in the corporate world. CMOs provided philanthropists an opportunity to earn a greater return on their donated dollar, not in financial profit but in substantial, observable societal improvement. The large footprint CMOs spread across multiple cities and even states provided philanthropists the best platform possible to make the greatest impact in educational reform. In comparison, the local, independently run chartered school had far less influence over public education as a whole. The CMO-philanthropist partnership, on the other hand, produced remarkable results. Within an astonishingly short time frame, CMOs were establishing multiple chartered schools that were rivaling and exceeding the outcomes of their traditional public school counterparts. Chartered schools were cropping up throughout our nation's urban centers and across states. They were providing parents searching for better public schools high-quality education beyond what these concerned moms and dads thought was possible.

Currently, CMOs are able to leverage their economies of scale to directly take on the challenges today's chartered schools face. In particular, combating pushback and pushback-related compliance burdens requires immense financial and human capital. Large, well-organized, and well-funded CMOs are best equipped to handle an increasingly regulated and scrutinized chartered school landscape. While scrappy, fiercely independent, and ambitious chartered schools have improved the lives of countless students across the nation, managing a successful program is becoming more complicated and expensive, and with pushback increasing rather than diminishing, chartered schools will face greater obstacles in the future.

Armed with their economies of scale, CMOs are bringing about rapid improvements to our nation's public schools. If you read *U.S. News & World Report*'s Best High Schools list, you will find CMO high schools at the top of the magazine's sought-after rankings. CMOs, such as BASIS, have raised the bar on the outcomes public schools are able to achieve. While top-performing CMOs are frequently criticized for an overemphasis on test preparation, they are universally recognized as well-run organizations that provide safe and welcoming environments for students and their parents.

In spite of the criticism by the educational establishment and others, we foresee CMOs at the forefront of educational reform.

Philanthropists realize their charity is best invested in organizations that have a track record of developing a solid educational model and bringing it to market. When philanthropists donate to CMOs, they do so believing their dollars will further strengthen already promising programs and thereby decrease the risk their patronage will be squandered. CMOs have created effective lobbying infrastructure that has compelled state and federal lawmakers to champion legislation that has further consolidated CMO dominance. This includes public funds earmarked for funding academically high-achieving schools, developing data-driven curricula, and new facility construction.

CMOs have also proven they are currently the most effective at protecting the interests of the educational reform movement within local, state, and federal legislatures. CMOs have created the strongest

mechanisms to fight pushback efforts from the educational establishment. Non-CMO chartered schools will fall behind their well-funded and
highly organized counterparts. They will find themselves in an increasingly competitive public education landscape, where they will lack the
resources and political power to defend themselves against pushback and
to influence local, state, and federal legislation. As CMOs continue on
their growth path, the educational establishment will further fortify their
pushback efforts. This will inevitably make it more expensive for small,
non-CMO chartered schools to combat pushback.

THREAT: Roles of Both Authorizers and Chartered Schools Are Changing

Over the course of the chartered school movement's twenty-five-year
history, the roles and responsibilities of both authorizers and chartered
schools have evolved. The biggest changes have taken place in states
where districts are the primary authorizing entity.

In the early years of the chartered school movement, school districts
charged with granting charters largely did so on a fair and neutral basis.
Their main objectives were to ensure chartered schools complied with
state and federal law and to develop procedures and policies to grant
charters. The arrangement was straightforward: The proposed chartered
school and the district authorizer were entering a contractual agreement
where the district would oversee the chartered school's operations.

The guiding oversight framework authorizers and chartered schools
would follow was the state-approved charter law. The level and quality of
charter law varied from state to state. Unlike today, school districts did
not view the chartered schools within their geographical boundaries as a
threat. At their onset, chartered schools were viewed with dispassionate
curiosity, and overseeing them was just one more item on a district's endless and ever-growing to-do list.

As far as the quality of oversight was concerned, some authorizers were
more diligent than others. On one end were authorizers that allocated the

least possible amount of time and money toward oversight. On the other end were school district authorizers that went to great lengths to ensure new chartered schools remained revenue neutral and in no way created a financial and legal liability for the school district.

The relationship between district authorizers and the chartered schools they oversaw continued on this nonantagonistic and even collaborative trajectory until districts identified an alarming trend: decreased student enrollment in the schools within their boundaries. Chartered schools were growing. Suddenly, chartered schools were a threat to a district's fiscal well-being. Now, they needed to be slowed, if not stopped altogether.

At the same time, as chartered schools continued to develop, district authorizers identified another threat: bad press. Reports of chartered school malfeasance, although isolated, reflected poorly on the entire burgeoning movement. The negative publicity moved upstream where authorizers' oversight was called into question. In other words, poorly managed chartered schools were creating public relations problems for district authorizers and harming their reputations. As a result, oversight took on greater importance.

Some district authorizers continued working with chartered schools in a collaborative spirit. Other district authorizers seized on the mandate for more stringent oversight as an opportunity to curb the movement that was taking away the district's market share. Authorizers leveraged their oversight duties for self-serving purposes. Even district authorizers in search of common ground with their chartered schools realized that these schools posed a threat.

About two decades after the nation's first charter laws were adopted, chartered schools had grown to the point where the educational establishment realized their continued success could spell disaster for many school districts. Districts located in urban areas were particularly at risk due to the large numbers of students enrolling in chartered schools. Districts around the country saw an impending fiscal crisis if traditional public schools continued losing market share from chartered schools.

By 2014, pushback became a highly organized, well-funded, and powerful strategy aimed at slowing and outright stopping chartered school growth. Armed with a pushback-driven agenda, authorizer oversight took a dark turn. Collaboration became adversarial. Regardless of the positive outcomes chartered schools demonstrated and the goodwill they earned among satisfied parents and students, the educational establishment declared them an enemy. An increasing number of authorizers became aggressive and hostile toward the chartered schools under their supervision.

While initially subtle, pushback galvanized into a well-funded and impeccably organized machine. Educational reformers, realizing their movement's future was at risk, built up their defenses. Pushback became an arms race, where both sides fortified their arsenals with lawyers, politicians, philanthropists, community members, and the media. Since then, one of the primary objectives of pushback is to force chartered schools to play by the same rules (that is, follow the same compliance framework) that guide traditional public schools.

Many in the educational establishment are determined to force chartered schools to be brought under the control of district authorizers and their superintendents. While some argue this would increase chartered school accountability, the underlying motive is often to slow the growth or eliminate chartered schools altogether. This version of pushback will most likely grow more virulent and forceful over time. What these pushback proponents seem to have forgotten is that, through their single-minded efforts to thwart the educational reform movement, the very students they are supposed to serve are often the collateral damage.

THREAT: An Evolving Compliance Model

In the future, as chartered schools continue on their growth trajectory, the rules governing them will most likely undergo restructuring. Under the current model, traditional public schools follow a state-mandated compliance framework. Chartered schools abide by charter school law, which is a different set of state-mandated rules. This "one public education system, two compliance frameworks" paradigm has led to pushback from the public education establishment. A frequent argument against chartered schools is that the traditional public school's compliance framework is far more onerous than charter school law.

Back in 1992, California's chartered schools were granted a megawaiver. This absolved them from most educational code, local district policy and procedure, and all negotiated contracts. The megawaiver preserved the independence that is the hallmark of the chartered school movement. Over time, this independence eroded. Educational reformers heard the sucking sound signaling the educational establishment was intent on drawing chartered schools into its web of educational code, local district policy and procedure, and negotiated contracts.

Megawaiver or no megawaiver, the educational establishment argues the relative simplicity of charter school law gives chartered schools more flexibility and autonomy, while the establishment flounders under a mountain of framework documentation. Because chartered schools are far less burdened, the establishment believes chartered schools have an unfair advantage, to the point where traditional public schools cannot compete fairly.

For example, traditional public schools and chartered schools follow separate human resources guidelines. Employee job descriptions and work hours and conditions are different. Traditional school employees are mostly unionized. Thus, job contracts are negotiated between school districts and unions. Chartered school employees can be either union or nonunion. If they are nonunion, employees usually work on an at-will basis. This is a legal designation for contractual relationships in which an employer can dismiss an employee for any reason and an employee can leave his or her job without reason or warning. Some nonunion chartered schools negotiate their employee contracts to include salary and benefit packages that can be worked out on an individual basis. In general, chartered school hiring guidelines provide their schools more flexibility when compared to the heavily bureaucratic practices traditional public schools must follow.

In the short term, chartered schools will most likely retain the option to have either a union or a nonunion workforce. But as chartered schools grow, the educational establishment will increase its pushback efforts. Authorizers will be charged with greater oversight authority, which could manifest itself in the increased regulation of chartered schools' hiring practices and encouragement of the unionization of its employees. Subjecting chartered schools to stricter hiring standards will diminish the flexibility that is a strength and hallmark of the chartered school movement. Rather than apply the hiring practices traditional schools must follow to chartered schools, traditional schools would benefit from implementing some of the effective practices of chartered schools. Over time, authorizers' stricter oversight authority may even extend beyond hiring and include chartered school operations, finance, and instruction.

As far as the "one public education system, two compliance frameworks" policy is concerned, in states with charter school law, this may be replaced by a single framework that both public education models follow. According to this approach, each state with charter school law would create a compliance framework that would regulate the operations of both types of public schools. In other words, the system of two compliance guidelines, which separates traditional public schools from chartered schools, may be replaced in states with chartered schools by a single compliance framework that both public education models follow.

Currently, many school districts take pride in the fact that both the traditional public schools and the chartered schools under their jurisdiction are evaluated by the same or a similar set of criteria. This is troubling for chartered schools because autonomy and freedom to innovate are the strengths that have resulted in the remarkable outcomes that have been their badge of honor. Forcing chartered schools to comply with rules that will constrict, if not fully block, their autonomy and freedom denies these unique schools a core part of their identity.

At first glance, a single regulatory model that applies to both seems an effective means to streamline public education and address unfairness. But scratch just slightly below the highly politicized public education surface and you will quickly realize that each state's compliance framework represents the agendas of the educational establishment, unions, special interests, and more. Thus, substantially modifying the traditional public education canon—let alone transitioning to a new model—would represent nothing less than a complete overhaul of America's public education system. But with the rapid expansion of chartered schools, their move from minnow to big fish, and the subsequent pushback from the educational establishment, the current two-set model of compliance guidelines may prove too unwieldy to maintain over time.

SWOT: The Educational Reform Movement's Past, Present, and Future

Throughout our cross-country investigation, we heard variations on the following theme: "Having a positive learning experience should not depend on your zip code." From the start, improving the existing public education model for students, regardless of where they live, has been at the heart of the educational reform movement's mission and purpose.

Only when students believe they are respected, supported, and safe and parents and community members have a voice can schools succeed in improving academic outcomes. The bottom line is public educators are in the people business, and their customers are parents, community members, and above all, students. Every day, chartered schools are charged with the enormous task of inspiring and enriching the lives of those the public educators serve.

In this chapter, we have provided you an overview that demonstrates the causal relationship between how chartered schools began, where they are presently, and how they will evolve in the future. As the educational reform movement continues to challenge the educational establishment, ever-increasing pushback will be the establishment's response. But chartered schools are not simply rolling over and recoiling from an attack that strikes at their very existence. Many chartered schools are:

- working closely with member organizations to professionally challenge districts that unreasonably deny them facilities or funding;

- acting as community organizers, earning parents' respect, and leveraging the parents' voices;

- resisting authorizers whose actions are illegal;

- "lawyering up" and pursing litigation;

- and aggressively lobbying officials who work at passing laws that support charters.

In addition, chartered schools and, specifically, CMOs have developed formidable marketing infrastructures. They are prepared to use their marketing might to defend against pushback and sway the court of public opinion in their favor. In this regard, traditional public education is at a significant disadvantage. Complacency and indifference have resulted in a mediocre to nonexistent marketing strategy that cannot compare with the robust public relations apparatus of many chartered schools, which are prepared to inform the public of what they offer and how they can meet student needs through means that most traditional public schools do not have.

Most importantly, the chartered school movement is proving unstoppable. As the saying goes, "Success breeds success." Individuals and organizations are supporting the educational reform movement in its growth and its defense against pushback. The underdog is ready to defend its purpose and mission, emboldened by its success and mandate and strengthened by public and philanthropic support that has only increased over time. Chartered schools have earned a permanent seat at the public education table. Pushback will continue, and the educational reform movement is ready to improve a flawed system and challenge the status quo.

Chapter 7

LESSONS LEARNED

BOSTON IS A city that values education. Its metropolitan area is an academic powerhouse with fifty-four institutions of higher education. The region has a thriving chartered school community that collaborates with the city's private and traditional public schools. During our Boston investigation, we met with top academics and public school leaders.

For example, we met with Charles L. Glenn and Roger Harris.

Glenn is professor emeritus of educational leadership at Boston University's School of Education. He is a prolific author and an authority on urban schooling, parental choice, religious education, and the history and sociology of education.

Harris is a clinical assistant professor at Boston University School of Education. He is also the president, CEO, and superintendent of Boston

Renaissance Charter Public School Foundation and a cofounder of the award-winning Roxbury Preparatory Charter School. As a foremost chartered school expert, he has earned numerous accolades, including the Change Maker Award from the Boston Foundation.

During our meeting, both education experts provided insight into the strengths and challenges of education reform in Boston, which boasts many of the nation's top chartered schools. The obstacles they described were ones that reflected Boston's historic roots. For example, many of the city's buildings have historic significance. This means strict preservation guidelines can prohibit chartered schools from making the changes required to run a legally compliant facility. Even if making necessary revisions were possible, implementing them is often cost-prohibitive.

In addition, the experts expressed that in the long run, the city's two-system public education model, comprising traditional public schools and chartered schools, would be fiscally unsustainable. In the end, only one will prevail. One possible future outcome is for chartered schools and traditional public schools to be guided and funded by the same system. Student-parent choice will most likely be the middle ground and long-term solution to address the problems arising from the current two-system structure.

"For the greater good, we need to share our successful programs and instruction with other charters. Currently, we do not have a process to do this," Harris said.

We could not agree more. For this reason, we have distilled the lessons we learned from our cross-country investigation, including discussions with educational leaders such as Glenn and Harris, into a prescription for action. We have identified the essential practices and steps necessary to strengthen individual chartered schools and the education reform movement as a whole. You will gain insight that will both guide and inform.

Create High-Performing Schools

All high-quality chartered schools share the same five-part formula: (1) five pillars of superb instructional programs; (2) amazing people within the organization; (3) strong financial capital; (4) safe, secure, and sustainable facilities; and (5) a solid strategic plan. Because the last two parts have interrelated elements, we will address them in one section.

Five Pillars of Superb Instructional Programs

The single greatest factor in evaluating the educational reform movement as a whole is how well chartered schools are meeting students' needs. A superb instructional program delivers an undeniably high-quality program that demonstrates positive outcomes through multiple measures. These include tracking the following five pillars:

1. Standardized test scores

2. Graduation, attendance, suspension, and expulsion rates

3. The performance of subgroups, including ethnic minorities and special education and socioeconomically disadvantaged populations

4. Cocurricular programs

5. Parental involvement

In addition, the community at large must believe the school is improving the lives of the students living within its boundaries. Last, a chartered school must receive the seal of approval from its evaluation or regulatory body, which includes any of the following: authorizers, school districts, the county, the state, and chartered school associations.

Central to a superb instructional program is a chartered school's commitment to aligning its curriculum and instruction to assessment. Chartered schools vary in their ability to commit to this important work. But aligning curriculum is critical for chartered schools to grow in the next decade. In order to accomplish this essential objective, chartered schools can participate in curriculum instruction workshops provided by their county office of education or hire consultants who are experts in curriculum instruction or both.

A prevailing myth is that chartered school curriculum is less rigorous than that of traditional public schools. Each chartered school must take it on itself to dispel this misconception. The positive results of standardized tests and other measures are key to proving that a school is instructionally sound.

Chartered schools that fall short of their responsibilities and consistently fail to meet students' needs should be quickly disavowed. With that said, for a chartered school to realize its bold vision often requires time. On the one hand, schools must be given the opportunity to develop the ambitious and rigorous programs they envision providing their students. On the other hand, schools that chronically underperform are not acting in students' best interests and should not be authorized to continue operations.

The bottom line is, for a school to call itself successful, it must have data to support its claim. Any school can say it runs a remarkable organization, but it must be able to quantify the quality of its instruction.

Amazing People within the Organization

Both the charter development group and the staff responsible for running the school every day are charged to execute the preceding five pillars. The charter development group's duty is to design and present an application to an authorizer. Members of the group often remain part of the chartered school as leaders or part of the governance board. They must have strong business expertise. The staff must be highly trained and qualified to meet their students' needs.

Strong Financial Capital

A fiscally strong chartered school provides operators with a budget that supports a start-up school and sufficient revenue to cover employee salary and benefits, facility acquisition, maintenance and operations, instructional

and technological needs, and all other costs required to adequately operate the business services associated with an instructional setting. Ideally, a
chartered school will also have access to enough capital to fund a strategic
reserve directed toward safeguarding against unforeseeable circumstances.

Safe, Secure, and Sustainable Facilities and a Solid Strategic Plan

Before the first student ever steps foot on campus, safe, secure, and sustainable facilities must be established. A chartered school's strategic plan
should be based on exhaustive research and designed around the demographics of the community it serves.

For decades, strategic planning has been an indispensable tool for
educational and business leaders. In its simplest terms, it is an examination of an organization's goals and the means to achieve them. It is also
a template for action for which the leadership can be held accountable.
The strategic plan identifies what an organization believes to be the most
important tasks that must be achieved. It outlines how goals, objectives,
and work plans will be implemented. Its function is to create a pathway
leaders will follow to maintain or improve their organizations. The strategic plan must be consistent with the organization's mission and vision
statements. It can address multiple areas, such as growth, personnel, budgets, facilities, transportation, research findings, political pitfalls, demographic change, economic trends, competitors' impact on growth and
development, legislation, and more. A strategic plan looks to the future.
It is a roadmap that considers one, three, and five years and beyond, and
it ensures a school maintains its long-term focus. It is not the same as a
business plan, which primarily addresses the start-up of an organization.

Without a strategic plan, a chartered school is doomed to fail over
the long term. For a school to succeed, it must have a strategic plan that
addresses its financial, instructional, and hiring objectives. In other words,
a school's vision is only as strong as its strategic plan. While strategic planning is often overlooked in many chartered schools' overall operations,
this must change. Running a successful program is hard work, but the day-
to-day responsibilities must move toward meeting larger goals.

Strategic planning helps chartered schools execute what sets them apart from traditional public schools. A strategic plan is essential for a chartered school to continually grow and improve and effectively protect and defend itself from pushback. Planning must be based on current data, emerging trends, and reasonable assumptions about the future. Strategic plans must reflect the organization as viewed by both internal and external stakeholders. All input and ideas must be considered in the development of this plan. Both strong supporters and naysayers hold valuable information that can bring the chartered school to a successful future. Armed with a strategic plan, a chartered school will boldly meet the challenges of a competitive public education marketplace in a way that reflects integrity, respect, and professionalism.

A strategic plan comprises realistic and measurable goals accepted by all stakeholders and must be continually reviewed and updated. It is not vague or informal. Rather, it is a clearly crafted document that ensures a chartered school realizes its mission. A well-developed strategic plan includes broad input from the community, how a school will determine it has met its goal and policies, and how each part of the plan will be funded.

In order for all stakeholders within a chartered school to uphold a strategic plan, they must be trained to both understand and follow it. Often, having staff members participate in its design is a powerful way to gain their insight and thereby increase their investment in implementing it. In addition, the strategic plan should account for how each department or division or both relate to the entire organization. This makes all stakeholders accountable to the whole. Key to an effective strategic plan is a chartered school leader who has initiative and a strong vision. This person has the intelligence and charisma to lead the school in the right direction.

Generally, a strategic plan will include foreseeable issues and concerns the organization must resolve. It can be written to address short-term goals (one to three years) or long-term goals that may take three to five years to implement. The plan is considered a living document, which means it can be adjusted as circumstances change within the organization. Because chartered schools are able to make quick course corrections, they are well suited to fulfill the strategic plan's objectives and fully experience its benefits.

Traditionally, the plan is revisited yearly, usually at the start of the new fiscal year. However, the specific work plans that flow from the goals must be monitored on a more frequent basis. Depending on the action or activity, this may require a monthly, weekly, or even daily check. The elements of the previous year's plan are evaluated for successful completion. Some elements not fully completed may be carried forward to full implementation. Elements identified as successfully completed can be eliminated from the plan. Newly identified needs and goals can be added to the current year plan. Many organizations prioritize the elements based on their needs or goals. The plan's elements may clearly identify whether the goals are oriented to feasibility, implementation, or full integration.

Sharing the plan with all staff provides a common vision driving the entire workforce along a collective and uniform pathway. Critical needs within the strategic plan have broad input from all stakeholders, all staff, numerous clients, various community members, major vendors, and other interested parties. A strategic plan's benefits include effective and efficient use of time, money, and labor with the greatest reward going to students attending a successful, well-run school with a clear vision and purposeful direction.

In larger organizations, a strategic-planning committee may report its findings to a top-level leadership team for input and approval. The committee will offer data to support its findings. Often a champion is named. This person is a leadership team member assigned to make certain all elements of the plan are implemented.

The strategic-plan format varies. It may be presented in written paragraph narrative with graphs and charts or a series of columns identifying goals, objectives, tasks, timelines, personnel, departments, and budget. Some organizations prefer that their strategic plan address only major initiatives including supporting elements. Other organizations combine major initiatives with current issues and concerns that will require substantial resources. The cost of implementation is always a key factor.

Elements of the plan—whether money, human capital, time, or evaluation—should be reflected in the annual budget.

These are the basic tenets of a strategic plan. Organizations striving for exceptional quality and high performance must consider strategic planning on a much more exhaustive and deeper level. This includes more specific and precise data, broader input, and perhaps the support and guidance of an outside consultant who has demonstrated that he or she can create or administer a high-performing organization. The internet is full of content on every facet and nuance of this subject. Elsewhere in this book, we have stated that a strategic plan is critical to any chartered school. It is unimaginable that a chartered school would not employ a well-prepared strategic plan to focus all its resources in a coordinated effort to meet its vision and mission in a timely and well-executed manner.

Crafting a high-quality strategic plan is a sophisticated skill. If a chartered school's leaders do not have the precise training necessary to develop one, they should consider seeking expert help to guide them in its development, execution, and regular review. With that stated, anyone can call himself or herself a strategic-planning consultant and charge huge fees for services. Within a chartered school, someone must be appointed to be responsible for researching the possible candidates and recommending someone with a truly credible track record.

Unite to Create a Greater Proactive Voice

As the educational reform movement has evolved, a new generation of leaders has emerged that is charged with carrying on the legacy of those who first boldly challenged the status quo. As you read previously, we refer to these founding leaders as the originals. Throughout the first decade of the chartered school movement, the originals helped design, develop, and pass charter school law and later established the first chartered schools.

The originals also include those that, while not part of the group that poured the legislative foundation of chartered schools, were early adopters who put educational reform into practice. Similar to what develops among any group of men and women involved in a start-up (whether it be a business, a volunteer organization, or a recreational sports team), the common purpose, hard work, reliance on one another, and rapid adjustment to change created deep and enduring bonds. Chartered school pioneers developed a camaraderie forged by facing common obstacles and celebrating victories together.

At their onset, chartered schools largely had only informal organizations and associations to rely on for support and resources. Under these fledgling circumstances, chartered schools counted mostly on each other to overcome the challenges of creating a new type of public school on a statewide scale. The originals knew that, in order for their individual schools to grow, they needed to be committed to both their campuses and the educational reform movement.

They understood the viability of chartered schools depended on supporting a long-term vision of public education that reflected their interests and values as a whole. Thus, the originals and the schools they supported would be best served by having a direct say in the laws that would shape their movement. Focusing on both their individual campuses and the overall movement was a formidable feat due to staffing and resource limitations. These limitations are common to all start-ups. School leaders and staff are often scrambling to meet their daily operational needs. The complexity is compounded by the fact that there are entities outside their own organizations that continually impose requirements and expectations.

The originals were visionaries. They boldly challenged the educational establishment and its overall reluctance and sometimes even outright refusal to embrace the innovations the chartered school model had developed. While many of the originals are still active in the chartered school movement, as of the time of this writing, many have retired, and new leaders have emerged.

Similar to the originals, the second generation of leaders includes brave men and women who are risk takers and who understand that to embrace educational reform often means to challenge the educational establishment. Whether these new leaders have a high level of expertise of the educational reform movement, they do have an unwavering passion to improve the lives of the students they serve. Most of these new leaders know a public school landscape only where pushback is the weapon the educational establishment wields in order to slow the growth of chartered schools or obliterate them altogether.

With a well-funded pushback machine growing in strength and intensity, now more than ever, everyone who supports educational reform—from chartered school staff to political leaders—must confront pushback with a strong, unified voice. With support systems at the local, state, and national level, the chartered school movement has established a solid foundation. But this pro–chartered school platform must grow and maintain a steadfast commitment to protect chartered schools against aggressive and relentless pushback. A fractured movement will easily succumb to pushback from the establishment, which is eager to pounce on any vulnerability with the full force of the educational establishment apparatus. It is only through a well-organized and shared mission that those on the front lines of educational reform can build a strong defense against pushback.

It has been a daunting task for educational reformers to maintain and build a unified structure powerful enough to defend itself against the educational establishment. Chartered schools are at a clear disadvantage when compared to their traditional public school counterparts. Here, independence and freedom, the hallmarks of the educational reform movement, can be problematic. Whereas all traditional public schools operate under a monolithic structure, chartered schools are much more loosely associated. The high volume of independently operating chartered schools has created a disjointed alliance. Without a strong and unified force, the movement risks becoming a victim of its own success. As chartered schools grow, the pitfalls associated with looser affiliations have grown as well. In the following section, we will address three threats to chartered school unity:

1. The large numbers and types of chartered schools

2. The widening ideological gap between CMO- and non-CMO-
    based chartered schools

3. The performance gap between chartered schools

The Large Numbers and Types of Chartered Schools

The originals worked in a small town–like chartered school landscape,
where nearly all chartered school leaders within a city or even a state
knew each other. They never imagined the boom that would spread over
the next two decades as chartered schools began opening their doors in
nearly every state.

Today, chartered schools are both widespread and diverse. With their
growth, new public educational models have emerged as well. With the
advent of virtual classrooms and independent-study programs, not all
chartered schools are site-based. While alternative educational programs
have previously existed, such as small home-study communities and
programs contained within traditional continuation-school structures,
chartered schools brought independent study and personalized education into the mainstream. States began adopting breakthrough programs
developed at the chartered school level.

Largely to the chagrin of the educational establishment, parents crav-
ing alternatives to public school offerings that were falling short of their
expectations eagerly enrolled their children in these innovative programs.
Today, the sheer number and types of chartered schools have made it
more difficult for chartered schools to build and maintain connections.
Each new model has its particular needs, which means that mutual interests have ebbed as differences have become greater. In some cases, the
agendas of different programs even conflict with each other.

The Widening Ideological Gap between CMO- and Non-CMO-Based Chartered Schools

Chartered management organizations presented an unintended intra-
educational reform movement challenge. Well-funded CMOs became the

public school equivalent of Starbucks and CVS. The independent non-CMO schools were like the locally owned coffeehouse and drugstore. With their economies of scale, CMOs threatened to drive out non-CMO chartered schools. With CMOs, non-CMO chartered schools, and traditional public schools sometimes competing in the same community, saturation inevitably emerged, and the CMO-based schools and traditional public schools had greater resources to stay afloat in a saturated market.

The disparate human and fiscal needs between CMO and non-CMO-based chartered schools resulted in both versions of chartered schools developing competing interests. These have threatened to fracture a common voice necessary to effectively combat pushback. New chartered schools are entering a matured public school marketplace, where they may be competing against established CMO-based and non-CMO-based chartered schools and traditional public schools. This can result in all public schools taking on an adversarial relationship with their competitors, an "every school for itself" perspective.

As the safety message before every flight says, "If you are traveling with a child or someone who requires assistance, secure your mask first, and then assist the other person." In the case of chartered schools, they too must look after their needs first. In other words, their top priority is to ensure they are operating their chartered school at a high standard. After all, a poorly running school does a disservice to its students and the educational reform movement as a whole. But once individual campuses are doing their best to serve their students, they must move beyond their walls and consider their place within public education. Advancing from taking care of themselves, they must now contribute to the greater educational reform movement. This step is vital to the continued success of all chartered schools.

Chartered schools must never lose sight of the long-term mission of their schools: putting children first by providing them the best public education possible. The only way to do this is to run amazing schools and support the greater cause. Both are the mandate of chartered schools. They will not survive by strengthening only one. Individual chartered schools,

CMO and non-CMO, must always remember they do not reside in a public school bubble. They cannot close their doors, so to speak, and ignore what takes place outside their classrooms and campuses. Pushback does not discriminate. Any chartered school that takes an isolationist point of view, where establishment pushback seems either irrelevant or inconsequential to a school's day-to-day operations, will most likely find itself unsuspecting prey in a ruthless pushback-driven public education setting.

All chartered school leaders must keep in mind that the goal of pushback is broad: slowing or dismantling the greater educational reform movement. But pushback is also narrow: tearing apart one campus at a time. Each chartered school's long-term viability and growth is contingent on a cohesive, committed effort to support and strengthen the educational reform movement as a whole.

The Performance Gap between Chartered Schools

Last, unity is threatened by the widening disparity between top-performing and underperforming chartered schools. While many chartered schools have exceeded their traditional public school counterparts in all standard achievement metrics, others have come up short. These poorly performing schools feed anti-educational reform arguments that say chartered schools are harming public education and threaten to steer public opinion against chartered schools.

Local and state chartered school associations and chartered schools must create a well-organized process to evaluate chartered school performance, encourage strong chartered schools, support struggling campuses filled with hardworking and highly motivated staff, and disavow schools that consistently fail to operate in their students' best interests.

While standardized tests are the most straightforward assessment tool to measure chartered school performance, these alone are insufficient, unfair, and imprecise. Test scores should play an important role in an evaluation process that is balanced and upholds the values that differentiate chartered schools from traditional public schools. With that said, evaluating schools beyond overly simplistic standardized test results—ones that fail to provide an accurate and detailed measure of a chartered school's strengths and weaknesses—is a daunting task.

Multiple factors influence a school's success. By design, chartered schools are charged to experiment and innovate, and all evaluation metrics must encourage rather than restrict chartered schools' distinct role in public education. Struggling schools working hard to meet their students' needs should be provided support, resources, and well-designed tools to evaluate their performance, as well as the time necessary to improve outcomes. Programs delivering consistently outstanding results should be given the freedom to evolve and grow and improve other chartered schools. In case after case, chartered schools have proven to be public education's best source of breakthrough pedagogy that meets the needs of a rapidly changing student population and the challenges all public schools face. Any effort to change how chartered schools operate must keep intact the structures that have made it possible for them to innovate.

Strength in Unity

The high numbers and types of chartered schools, the widening ideological gap between CMO-based and non-CMO-based chartered schools, and the performance gap between chartered schools are all potential barriers to educational reform movement solidarity. Despite these significant obstacles, it is only through joining forces in a singular voice that chartered schools will maintain their autonomy and flexibility and successfully defend against pushback.

Together, chartered schools must work to elevate all school standards by promoting and embracing research and supporting educational organizations. Research refers to the chartered schools' need to pursue quality programs and outcomes. This type of research requires an openness to sharing successful instructional, operational, and organizational practices.

The term "educational organizations" refers to the national, state, and local level chartered school membership associations that provide professional development for their members, advocate for a fair and balanced application of laws relating to chartered schools, and support a dynamic and vibrant lobbying effort focused on the creation of pro–charter school law.

In California, one such educational association is the Charter Schools Development Center, which is led by Eric Premack, one of the originals. He is an educational reform leader who was central to the efforts of Gary Hart, the former California state senator credited with passing the Golden State's charter law in 1992.

Nationally, Premack is known for the work he has done lobbying for strong charter law and tirelessly working on behalf of individual chartered schools facing pushback from authorizers and other educational establishment forces bent on slowing chartered school growth. An intellectually gifted leader and warrior for the educational reform movement, Premack has provided a bold, process-oriented approach to negotiation, rooted in a broad knowledge of education code, charter law, finance, and the political process affecting public education.

Ted Kolderie, another original, has influenced Premack. Kolderie is cofounder of Education Evolving and the originator of the first charter law in the United States. Respected for his articulate and thoughtful advocacy, Premack founded and directs a charter association that is a model for strong educational leadership. As chartered schools continue to grow and develop, the educational reform movement has Kolderie to thank for its success as a start-up, grassroots movement. Originals, such as Premack and Kolderie, have led the educational reform movement by introducing new, innovative pedagogy and providing a moral compass.

Only through a combined effort can chartered schools reach their lofty goals. No one school alone can accomplish these objectives over the long term. Chartered schools that engage in isolationism are taking a shortsighted perspective. By doing so, they are putting their future and the educational reform movement's future at risk. Instead, by standing behind a common agenda that is strong, clearly articulated, and well designed, all chartered schools and, most importantly, students across the nation benefit.

Manage the Parent's Voice

Whether an individual chartered school realizes it, it is tied to an entire movement. The triumphs and failures of one school affect public perception of all schools. The educational establishment, and its powerful public relations apparatus, typically rejects highlighting the accomplishments of chartered schools and is more than eager to pounce on any chartered school malfeasance, regardless of its veracity or lack thereof.

Parents play a critical role in strengthening chartered schools. Next to students, parents are those that most benefit from the promise of educational reform. Their collective voice of support lends immense credibility to the movement and influences public opinion. Positive public opinion translates to priceless political capital that the educational reform movement can leverage to further its mission. Parents are also a persuasive voice that can directly influence legislators to advocate on behalf of chartered schools.

One example where chartered schools would benefit from a well-organized parental voice is funding. For chartered schools to thrive in the long term, they must maintain and stabilize their long-term funding status at every level in every state. They must reject the position most school districts maintain: Funding belongs to districts, and districts are charged with sharing it with the chartered schools they authorize. Instead, chartered schools must stand behind a fiscal approach where funding is attached to each student. This is a direct-funding model, which implies the state's funding of chartered schools is allocated to the chartered school rather than to another entity, such as an authorizer. Direct funding is the only way to fully realize a market-driven model of public education. Unfortunately, the absence of direct funding has slowed the efforts of educational reformers.

Chartered schools have the responsibility to motivate and give parents the tools to effectively express their support of their local schools, as well as the educational reform movement as a whole. Leaders within individual chartered schools must have an active and targeted plan to inform parents of political issues and concerns that directly affect their children.

The harsh reality is that, without strong and unified parental support, the educational reform movement will not survive pushback. The inverse is true as well. Arming parents with a well-organized and compelling voice is a powerful weapon to combat pushback. When parents see the amazing work chartered schools perform every day to meet their children's needs, they are often eager to advocate on behalf of their schools. It is the school's duty to make the most of this pro-chartered energy and enthusiasm by providing parents the resources they need to be effective spokespeople.

A parent's socioeconomic background or limitations in communicating in English must never be the reason his or her voice of support is not leveraged. For example, if a translator is needed, then a school should do its utmost to provide one. Every parent's voice deserves to be given equal value and weight in decision-making. Here is where chartered schools have been far more successful than traditional public schools.

In many school board meetings across the country, the parent's voice, when expressing a desire for change or opposition to a particular decision, has been silenced. In contrast, throughout their history, chartered schools have welcomed the parent voice. Supportive opinions have signaled a job done well, and dissent has marked areas where schools can improve. For chartered schools, change is embraced rather than rejected or feared. This creates an environment that encourages parents' input.

While suppressing the parent's voice in the short term may meet a school district's objectives, over time this strategy will backfire. Districts wind up losing credibility and respect within the communities they are ostensibly charged with serving. Proponents of educational reform are all too happy to seize on this weakness to offer programs parents seek for their children.

With that said, being a champion for the parent's voice is a formidable task. Parents who are passionate about their points of view can become steadfast and aggressive in expressing their perspectives. While well intentioned, an overly zealous attitude can do more harm than good when it comes to persuading the public.

Parents are relying on chartered school leaders to guide them. At all times, chartered school leaders must be impeccable role models who demonstrate respect and calmness. They must be skilled facilitators who know how to engender professionalism and courtesy. Part of this requires chartered school leaders to fully understand the issues at stake. They must be well versed in a particular position and have developed skilled arguments and counterarguments. Leaders must then effectively transfer this knowledge to parents and prepare them to persuasively deliver their points of view.

State chartered school associations are the key to training chartered school leaders and parents to express their support for educational reform in the most effective way possible. The stronger a state's charter school law and chartered school association, the more resources member chartered schools have to identify the issues that are at the forefront of public education. Many tools exist to evaluate the strength of each state's charter school law. The National Alliance for Public Charter Schools and the Center for Education Reform both provide information regarding the state of chartered schools across the country. Educational reform leaders should identify which laws work in their favor and which should be revised.

Authorizer Overreach

As is the case with many large organizations spread across the country, traditional public schools vary in quality from region to region. Some traditional public schools do remarkable work every day, while others fail miserably. Chartered schools are no different. They too vary in quality from one campus to another.

Authorizers play an important role in upholding chartered school accountability. They must do everything in their power to shut down chartered schools that are providing poor instruction, demonstrating fiscal irresponsibility, neglecting to meet students' and parents' needs, and mismanaging their operations. With that said, if a school would benefit from support and time to improve, then an authorizer should do whatever it can to provide the school the resources it needs to improve. A spirit of teamwork and collaboration is mutually beneficial and, in the end, improves students' lives.

But if the educational establishment exerts pressure on authorizers to fulfill their duties in a way that results in unfair oversight and perhaps even bullying chartered schools, then chartered schools must be willing and prepared to defend themselves. In too many instances, authorizers have overreached their authority. For example, a particular chartered school practice may have been in place for years without issue. The authorizer both sanctioned and supported it. Suddenly, the authorizer has chosen to apply a strict (and often inaccurate) interpretation of statutory law to crack down on previously acceptable practices.

Across the country, the educational establishment is pressuring authorizers to reinterpret past policies, practices, and procedures often under the guise of increasing accountability. What their efforts actually signal, however, is an effort to slow chartered school growth and move chartered schools closer to the traditional public school model. In other words, the educational establishment seeks to limit, if not completely abolish, the hallmarks of chartered schools: flexibility and autonomy.

At their onset, chartered schools were neither a threat nor a target of scrutiny by the educational establishment. But as they have grown and depleted market share of traditional public schools, school districts have taken notice of shrinking district revenue. Suddenly, chartered schools that had been compliant with charter law, responsibly used tax dollars to educate their students, and loyally served their communities were now being overseen with unprecedented scrutiny. School districts and their authorizers shared their pushback strategies with one another, and more and more chartered schools fell prey to overzealous oversight.

Educational reformers must unite to combat the well-oiled pushback machine. No matter how aggressive pushback is, chartered schools must be steadfast in their commitment to dismantle the exclusive franchise traditional school districts have held. When one chartered school is

unfairly attacked, this move threatens all chartered schools. When a chartered school focuses only inward—in other words, only on the needs of
its campus—this threatens the long-term future of the school itself and
the entire educational reform movement. For the health of all chartered
schools, when one school falls prey to pushback, it behooves all chartered
schools to sit up and pay attention.

Here is where flexibility and autonomy could be weaknesses. The
very independence that makes chartered schools remarkable institutions
for change could also make them diminish the importance they place on
the greater educational reform movement. A chartered school community lacking cohesion makes all chartered schools vulnerable to pushback.
Although each chartered school has its distinct identity, it must always
maintain its connection to the whole.

From the local level to the state and national levels, chartered school
communities must maintain a consistently strong voice that is well
informed, well organized, and skilled at public relations. Community and
state chartered associations need all schools to participate to effectively
maintain strong educational reform advocacy.

Divide and conquer is clearly the educational establishment's pushback *modus operandi.* Intimidation through threats of revoking authorization is a powerful weapon to dismantle the vision of educational reformers. Personal reputations are attacked and sometimes destroyed under the
pretense of exposing wrongdoing. Pushback is specific and broad as well
as subtle and explicit. It targets individual schools and the entire educational reform movement. Under these adverse circumstances, the only
way chartered schools can survive is through developing and executing a
strategic plan to combat pushback. Chartered schools should never surrender their values and legal rights for the sake of cooling a heated authorizer relationship.

With that said, our cross-country research revealed many authorizer-
chartered school partnerships that reflected mutual respect. Issues that
arose were resolved through negotiation and compromise. This is the way
the authorizer–chartered school relationship should be: Both entities

treat each another as equals and put professionalism and the needs of students at the forefront.

Engage the Media

The media play a central role in shaping public opinion. Broadcast, online, and print news have the power to set editorial policy that harms or supports a particular point of view. For the most part, reporters do not outright lie in their stories. However, the manner in which they organize their stories and present their arguments can persuade readers to interpret information favoring one side versus another.

In the case of public education, in many instances and on both a local and national level, media outlets and news reporters have a long-standing relationship with those within the educational establishment. Both have an agenda: Those within the educational establishment seek media coverage that supports and highlights its benefit to society, and media outlets and reporters seek newsworthy content. When the two feed off each other without thorough fact-checking and within communities where chartered schools are growing, this usually spells trouble for chartered schools. As the saying goes, "There are two sides to every story." Fair and balanced media coverage requires reporters to account for two opposing perspectives of a particular event. Too often, however, the educational establishment receives favorable coverage to the detriment of the educational reform movement. Every effort must be made to offer two fair and objective perspectives.

The media is in perpetual search for a story that will generate reader interest, which will increase advertising revenue. Even in cases where a story seems to lack an interesting angle, one can be created. The point is that, while an article may be presented as objective, this may not always be the case. In fact, opinion and bias are not restricted to a publication's editorial page; they regularly make their way to the news and features sections. Sometimes this bias is pro–educational reform. In most instances, however, the educational establishment has successfully leveraged the media as a pushback instrument. There are exceptions. Within some communities, traditional public schools have consistently underperformed. In these cases, when parental dissatisfaction is high and the educational establishment malfeasance is egregious, a community's chartered schools have a higher likelihood of receiving positive media coverage. Thus, chartered schools must have a well-developed public relations strategy to leverage positive media opportunities.

For the educational reform movement to thrive, each chartered school must have a plan to engage the media. Skillfully doing so requires a well-thought-out strategy that should never be haphazard. Unfortunately, many chartered school operators are unfamiliar with how to deal with the media. Adding another to-do item to an already long list of day-to-day responsibilities is a formidable requirement. But for chartered schools to thrive in the long run, a media plan is imperative.

No doubt, working with the media is challenging. It is, however, a learned skill that, once mastered, will greatly benefit an individual chartered school, as well as the educational reform movement as a whole. Continually investing in building relationships with the media is an important way to highlight how chartered schools are improving public education. Over time, this will increase public support of chartered schools.

Fundamental Steps to Engaging the Media

For a chartered school's long-term success, self-promotion is nonnegotiable. If a school has a great program, then it must skillfully communicate this to the public at large. In most instances, the most efficient and effective way to do this is through engaging the media. The best school programs in the world are fruitless if the media is uninformed, disinterested, and disengaged. Thus, it is the chartered school's responsibility to inform, generate interest, and engage the media. In rare instances, chartered schools will gain positive media coverage with no effort. But in most cases, being featured or referenced positively in a story requires developing a publicity plan and executing it.

Schools that have remarkable outcomes have the most compelling stories to tell and are the best equipped to engage the media. The following are basic steps. Keep in mind this section is intended to point out the importance of actively engaging the media. This is by no means a comprehensive guide to creating a public relations strategy.

Know Your School

Have you identified your mission, vision, and program? Only when you know your school can you have an informed and articulate discussion about it—one that is credible and interesting. Reporters want facts and interesting stories. If you have impressive academic performance metrics, then be prepared to share these. If you have stories of staff or students overcoming adversity as a result of being part of an amazing school community, be ready to describe these.

Identify Local Media Outlets

Find community newspapers and magazines, begin opening lines of communication with their staff, and then, maintain these connections over the long term. You must always build relationships. This is not a one-time effort. Over months and even years, you may have developed a close professional relationship with reporters, only to find out they have left their posts to take jobs in new cities. Your responsibility is to find out who their replacements are and develop a relationship with them.

Generate Content

Local publications are always seeking interesting content. Whether the news is positive or negative, they are always looking for a story to tell. Consider ways to highlight the positive in thoughtful, well-written news releases. Always think of how you can point out the wonderful work taking place on your campus that will strengthen the educational reform movement as a whole.

In whatever content you produce, always uphold copyright and privacy laws. This means any images you use, whether stock photos or those of students or parents, must be legally compliant. You can run into trouble if you use images without receiving proper authorizations or approvals first.

Consider Hiring an Expert

Engaging the media effectively often requires third-party professional support. Whether a chartered school hires public relations and marketing firms or handles publicity in-house, chartered schools must develop a thoughtful media strategy that is consistent over the long term.

Summary

The media can be a friend or foe or both. Sometimes being a foe is unavoidable. In many instances, however, a tense relationship with the media can be prevented or ameliorated if chartered schools make effectively engaging the media a high priority. Chartered schools must master the skills necessary to work with the media, mitigate negative stories, and gain coverage on the important work they do in the community.

Seek Legal Representation

When hiring lawyers, be sure they understand and will represent your chartered school management style, as well as your educational reform perspective. Chartered school operators should seek to have a clear understanding of the existing policies, practices, and procedures that affect their schools. The reality, however, is this is nearly impossible because these are subject to interpretation. We encourage chartered school operators to seek a flexible interpretation of existing policies, practices, and procedures and not tolerate a district's interpretation when it is self-serving and intended to be used as a pushback weapon. The educational reform movement benefits from the latter type of operators because without them, the educational establishment would succeed in its pushback objectives.

These days, lawyers representing chartered schools may work for firms representing a school district on a similar issue. This may represent a conflict of interest on the part of the law firm. With that said, determining conflicts of interest is not always clear-cut. Today, you will find more law firms specializing in representing chartered schools. A well-thought-out and researched selection of legal representation may avoid a serious conflict of interest.

Well-seasoned chartered school leaders collaborate with their legal representation, listening to counsel and evaluating the advice. Since leaders and their support staff are much better informed about their school circumstances and desired outcomes, they weigh the guidance from their lawyers against that knowledge. However, move with caution. Beware of disregarding legal advice. School boards, communities, and staff judge harshly if your decision-making is perceived to be based on your heightened emotional state, or you are simply wrong in disregarding your legal advisors.

Lobby for Legislation That Supports the Educational Reform Movement's Objectives

Learn how your chartered school can influence legislation that supports the educational reform movement, which, over the long term, will benefit your school. Pushback from the educational establishment is aggressive and often unreasonable and outright illegal.

For example, taking a bold stand against funding inequity is an important way to ensure that chartered schools remain viable for years to come. "Across the nation, charter schools continuously get cheated out of resources, even in places like the District of Columbia where charter schools currently serve as the educational lifeline for 44 percent of the public school population," said Kara Kerwin, president of the Center for Education Reform. Continued inequity and policy ignorance harms chartered schools and the students they serve. Other areas that require vigilance include risks to chartered school flexibility and autonomy and access to facilities. Understanding the issues and working together with others at the forefront of educational reform is key to effectively supporting and creating pro–chartered school legislation.

Develop and Grow State-Level Associations

Out of fifty states, thirty-two have statewide chartered school associations. State associations act as a collective voice for the chartered schools. Highly professional and well-funded associations help member chartered schools create top-performing academic programs. These associations advocate for policies that protect school operations and enforce pro–charter school laws. Strong and active associations can attract funding from philanthropists looking to make a difference in society.

In our research, states with healthy chartered school associations tend to have:

- strong pro–charter school laws;

- exemplary chartered schools;

- educational reform leadership that feels more secure about the future well-being of chartered schools;

- and robust member outreach.

For example, during our visit in Colorado, we met Nora Flood, a superb chartered school leader. She was then the president of the Colorado League of Charter Schools, which is a nonprofit membership organization that supports chartered schools statewide and is the state's largest educational institution. In 2013, a year before our meeting with Flood, Colorado had 210 chartered schools that served ninety-six thousand students, which represented 11 percent of the state's student population. The group assists chartered schools with applications, contract negotiations, and start-up and provides technical and legal support, public relations services, and resources to improve student performance.

Develop Resources Supporting Litigation That Clarifies Charter Law

Chartered school state associations must continue to engage philanthropists that support the educational reform movement. Philanthropist backing is how existing charter school law, which at present is generally vague and exposes chartered schools to pushback, will continue to move in a direction that promotes innovation and creativity rather than adding further restriction. One of the objectives of pushback is to strip chartered schools of their autonomy and bind them to a more traditional compliance framework.

In our investigation, we observed that chartered schools that have found their voice are still limited in number. As the educational reform movement grows, the voices of parents, chartered school leadership, and community members will have the greatest impact when combined with heavy investment in legislation, political action, and litigation that supports chartered schools.

An example of litigation that clarifies charter school law would relate to the organizational status of chartered schools. At one point, chartered schools were encouraged to become public corporations. One of the reasons to do this was to reduce the authorizer's legal liability. If, in the future, chartered schools and traditional public schools operate under the same guidelines, chartered schools' public corporation status will most likely change because such a status would be incompatible with traditional public schools. Chartered schools and traditional public schools have always been two distinct models for public education. From the start, chartered schools were designed to operate differently than traditional public schools. For chartered schools to continue their remarkable work, laws must uphold their independence and their ability to innovate.

Support Pro-educational Reform Legislators

Legislators who value educational reform are essential to the long-term success of chartered schools. They are advocates who will vote in favor of establishing more chartered schools and pro-chartered legislation. So how do you assess the educational reform stance of a particular lawmaker?

First, research his or her voting record when it comes to charter funding and autonomy legislation. Use this information to determine how you will craft your outreach strategy. Unless you perform research ahead of time, your efforts risk being irrelevant or ineffective.

Second, meet with legislators at the local, state, and even national level. Your voice will contribute to their understanding of the role of educational reform in our nation's public education system. Your face-to-face time will also help you to gain firsthand knowledge in how the political process works. As a result, you will be a better educational reform advocate. The bottom line is not always how you legislate or promote a particular concept. Rather, it is how the legislator votes.

Prepare for More Market Share . . . and More Pushback

Previously in this chapter, you read about the originals, the founding leaders of the educational reform movement. Not even these visionaries imagined chartered schools would grow to the point where they would take away significant market share from traditional public schools. In fact, they generally believed chartered schools would be a small category of public school that would leverage their independence to innovate. Traditional public schools would gain insight from chartered schools to improve education for all. In this way, chartered schools were laboratories for learning.

Fast-forward to today. Chartered schools have spread across the country, sometimes competing head-to-head with traditional public schools and often generating student waiting lists. As demand outgrows supply, chartered schools must figure out how to educate a population of students desperately in need of safe, high-quality schools.

Despite this demand, under the current system, chartered schools are not treated with the fairness and respect they have earned and are their right. If chartered schools must apply to the state for authorization, it would make sense to develop a similar process for facilities. Such a program could lead to the establishment of a state commission in states that oversee equitable funding, facilities allocation, and credentialing. Some states already have multiple authorizers or state commissions that manage multiple chartered school issues. Chartered school developers would first apply for an authorization to start a school. Obtaining approval would imply acceptance of the instructional plan supported by state funding. The chartered school developers would be expected to notify the school district of their intentions to operate a new school within the district's boundaries.

Overall, the bureaucracy, expense, and hurdles required to establish facilities explain why some chartered schools have been authorized but have never opened their doors. Consider issues related to instructional assessment and choices, governance, funding, transportation, staffing, special education, and multiple other requirements that are often outside charter law. Clearly, today's chartered schools are barraged with carefully orchestrated constraints that only increase with time.

The educational establishment and its operatives often claim the high regulatory barriers are intended to identify and shut down poorly performing chartered schools. No doubt, low-quality chartered schools exist. But every time one subpar chartered school is identified, often a series of new regulations is introduced. These only create additional bureaucratic hurdles for the vast majority of schools doing exemplary work every day.

To take a balanced perspective, let us explore what occurs within traditional public education. Poorly performing traditional public schools far outnumber underperforming chartered schools. But when it comes to malfeasance on the part of a traditional school or even an entire school district, rarely are laws introduced that affect all public schools. An errant traditional public school may undergo "restructuring," a nebulous term that may require a school to take drastic action or no action at all. In contrast, a subpar chartered school may have its charter revoked.

In fact, traditional schools are rarely closed for poor performance. If they are shuttered, the most frequent reason is they are underenrolled, which is often referred to as underresourced. These schools are generally located in socioeconomically poor areas that serve minority populations. While underresourced schools may be a financial burden for the school district, closing them would limit the public education options for students most in need of quality public schools. The double standard applied to under-performing chartered schools and traditional public schools is undeniable.

Chartered Schools Have Broken the Mold

When traditional public schools are criticized for maintaining the ped-agogical status quo despite changing student demographics or under-performance or both, the educational establishment points to ambitious reforms such as No Child Left Behind and Common Core. With both of these programs, curriculum and instruction were immortalized within written guidelines and handbooks. Teachers were given specific instruc-tional methodology that included sample lessons, sample outlines, and countless hours of teacher training in the latest pedagogy. Administra-tors were also trained to evaluate teachers within these new guidelines. Traditional education was marketed as forward thinking and aggressively working toward enhancing the learning experience.

One objective of these reforms was to replace the tried-and-true method where a teacher stood up and lectured to a class with individualized instruc-tion. Despite these efforts to change, if you go into most K–12 classrooms today, you will find the majority of time is still spent with the teacher stand-ing front and center of the classroom, lecturing the students. Although the educational establishment promotes itself as an institution that embraces innovation, the truth is it is steeped in status quo. In fact, many critics of traditional public education argue little instructional change has taken place inside the classroom despite claims to the contrary.

The bottom line is more resources do not necessarily create innova-tion, change, or dramatic improvement. In other words, the quantity of student learning has not dramatically changed. Rather, what continually changes is how we assess learning and how we use that information. In the end, these efforts largely maintain the status quo and demonstrate its supposed success. The primary reason this condition continues to exist is there is no long-term state or national educational instructional and assessment plan. What winds up happening instead is traditional public schools follow the latest educational theory, and once that approach is declared passé, so goes the instructional design. Then, it is onto the next "greatest and latest."

A continuing problem in traditional public education is how grants and specially funded programs are eliminated without ever reaching maturity. Often, the stated benefits for which the concept was funded fail to mature in either participation or time. More often than not, there is never a final evaluation to determine the degree of success based on student achievement. The practice is to simply end the benefit when the funding runs out and move on to whatever is funded next.

Chartered schools came along and broke the mold. They developed and promulgated individualized learning, virtual learning, and blended models and continue to create cutting-edge approaches ready to prepare a rapidly changing student landscape. Chartered schools have shifted the focus from centralized school results to individual student growth and results.

In this chapter, we have discussed the results of our cross-country research and highlighted what leads to lasting success for chartered schools. By following this prescription for action, you will be better equipped to face the obstacles that lie ahead. You will effectively challenge the status quo and develop and implement the breakthrough strategies that are chartered schools' legacy and strength and have forever improved public education.

Chapter 8

PHILANTHROPY

IN 2016, THE Irvine Company, led by billionaire Donald Bren, pledged twenty million dollars to the fine arts, music, and science programs of the Irvine Unified School District in Orange County, California. In front of a crowd of 150 teachers, parents, and district staff, Robin Leftwhich, Irvine Company's vice president of community affairs, made the donation announcement. A standing ovation from the audience ensued.

"This gift from Irvine Co. allows us to continue an enrichment program that distinguishes Irvine schools nationally," said Irvine Unified School District superintendent Terry Walker. According to the Irvine Company, Bren and his real estate business have donated more than $220 million to support education in Irvine.

Administrators, teachers, parents, and students were thrilled to receive the most recent twenty-million-dollar donation. While not every district in the country benefits from such philanthropic largesse, the Irvine Company example is one among countless that demonstrates the private sector–public sector ties that are common in public education.

Philanthropy is defined as "the desire to promote the welfare of others, expressed especially by the generous donation of money to good causes." The role of philanthropy in public life is deeply embedded within both past and present US culture. From museums to libraries, philanthropists have supported and even fully funded the nation's most vital public institutions. Throughout our country's history, philanthropists have used their wealth to leave their mark on society, ensuring their bold visions of an improved public life became reality.

In particular, the philanthropy-education connection has been an enduring partnership that, for generations, has promulgated the promise of preparing the hearts and minds of the masses.

Today, the relationship between philanthropy and public education is under fire. Specifically, many in the educational establishment have been outspoken critics of the role of philanthropy in the educational reform movement. A frequent argument levied against this relationship is the concern that for-profit organizations and chartered schools are converting public funds into private money. In other words, philanthropic donations to chartered schools are actually supporting a for-profit conspiracy.

There Is No Conspiracy

Throughout all layers of government, the purchase of private-sector services and goods is common practice. Public money cycling into private money is both ordinary and enduring. In fact, government contracts constitute the revenue backbone of many of the country's most well-respected and successful corporations. Thus, the notion that chartered schools and private entities are somehow colluding with each other in an unprecedented alliance and damaging public education in the process is a misguided illusion.

Public education is complicated and highly regulated, and unfortunately, those conditions also make it extremely expensive. Traditional public schools and chartered schools regularly purchase goods and services from for-profit corporations. From buying textbooks and technology to purchasing paper and pencils, all public schools engage in this long-standing practice; thankfully, the right choice of vendor can often cut costs and increase operational efficiency. In addition to buying necessities from private businesses, most public high school athletic departments have boosters that set up foundations that receive monies from a variety of public and private sources. They are free to expend funds that benefit student athletic activities.

Suddenly, however, when a chartered school hires a third-party back-office service to manage payroll, accounting, human resources, audits, or filing of government documents, the educational establishment cries foul. The establishment has deemed itself the unofficial and somehow impartial arbiter to determine the proper relationship between the public and private sectors. Far from impartial, the blatantly biased perspectives and arguments coming from the establishment make their criticisms crumble into spurious nit-picking rather than well-formed analysis.

When traditional public schools contract with private industry, the relationship is for the public good and is accepted without impunity. The educational establishment declares that chartered schools are privatizing our cherished schools and scheming with the dark forces of corporate America. The establishment contends that philanthropists, many of whom are leaders of successful businesses, are meddling out of gain-oriented self-interest to the detriment of public schools. Under current anti–chartered school polemics, CMOs are the primary target of this type of pushback.

In many instances, CMOs are the founding entities that develop and launch one chartered school or, more often, a series of them. Similar to the business practice championed by corporate America, CMOs leverage economies of scale to chartered schools' benefit. Schools linked together buy materials and services in high volume and consequently at a discount—the more they buy, the lower the per-item cost. In the case of CMOs, decreased expenses result in more resources directed toward serving chartered school students.

A chartered school may purchase third-party back-office services or consultative services—just as traditional public schools may do. A chartered school's decision to hire a particular company is voluntary and may be based on multiple factors. This relationship may greatly benefit the school and allow much more flexibility.

Abuse of this flexibility is one of the factors behind the educational establishment's criticisms of chartered schools. The establishment points to examples of chartered schools that have taken what it deems excessive amounts from their accounts to pay for generalized or unexplained expenses. Furthermore, the establishment argues that the corporate dollars or services comingled with chartered schools come with strings attached.

When authorizers raise questions regarding those funds, the educational establishment contends CMOs provide inadequate answers. In critics' minds, the use of public funds must be open to public disclosure. In most cases, CMOs' private, nonprofit corporate status means they are not legally required to report their accounting to chartered school authorizers. By law, chartered school fiscal accounting is subject to auditing and authorizer inspection. Local and state public education officials regularly examine chartered schools' books. Authorizers are charged with expressing concern over possible conflicts of interest they have identified. Thus, the real issue here is one of governance, where authorizers must keep an eye out for dishonest outliers trying to take advantage of the chartered school system, rather than of a defective paradigm. Opponents would have chartered schools leashed into the limiting traditional educational compliance model. But when countless CMOs are practicing sound and ethical accounting, it is unfair to punish all chartered schools for the malfeasance of a few.

Conflicts often arise from the complicated relationship between chartered schools, CMOs, and authorizers—a historically unprecedented public education triad. Unfortunately, simple comparisons do not accurately describe the complex relationship between chartered schools, CMOs, and authorizers. A two-way, buyer-vendor relationship is not the same as the three-part (i.e., chartered school, CMO, and authorizer) arrangement.

For example, when chartered schools buy merchandise from book or furniture dealers or technology from private, for-profit entities, the authorizer is not privy to the seller's accounting records. A chartered school board of directors has the freedom to make independent choices as far as how it runs its schools. If it chooses to hire private nonprofit or private for-profit organizations, that is both its right and its decision, which may be based on providing the school a fiscal benefit. As we have mentioned before, adequate education is not simple or cheap.

As you have learned throughout this book, traditional public education moves at a snail's pace. Change comes slowly, and anything outside long-established practices is viewed with doubt and often hostility. Instead of offering nuanced and sophisticated solutions to address weaknesses the educational establishment has identified within chartered schools, the establishment is wont to propose controlling measures. These are often more examples of pushback rather than a genuine interest in improving an evolving public education model.

While many of the chartered school–private organization relationships are positive, for-profit entities managing chartered schools tend to be more problematic. Those opposed to this type of arrangement often fiercely object to companies profiting from offering critically important, publicly funded services to children. They raise worst-case scenarios in which shareholder demands would come before meeting student needs. While on the surface this argument is compelling, it neglects to highlight the important role authorizers play in overseeing chartered school operations.

Both the educational reform movement and the establishment benefit from innovation. In many instances, a for-profit company may be the best entity poised to provide an entirely new approach that will improve student outcomes. Thus, cutting off all possibilities, at the risk of losing innovative strategies, would not address public education's most pressing need: to put students first. When authorizers use their power to stop practices that are noncompliant and encourage those that benefit students, they raise the standards by which all public schools are measured.

Philanthropic Donations: A Double Standard?

The educational establishment's overall message is a variation on the following: Philanthropists are damaging this sacred public institution. While no empirical evidence exists to substantiate this argument, this does not stop antiphilanthropic forces within the establishment from stooping to name-calling to perpetuate their claims. Advocates of the philanthropy–chartered school partnership are called neoliberals, educational capitalists, corporate educationalists, institutional entrepreneurs, and privatizationalists.

What is often absent from this critique is how philanthropy receives little to no scrutiny when the patrons are supporting traditional public schools. Districts across the country benefit from grants, financial gifts, and privately funded programs. For generations, car manufacturers have donated vehicles to high school auto shop programs, small local businesses have sponsored school events, and philanthropists have donated funds to build gymnasiums, football fields, and science labs, as well as supported music and technology programs. These gifts were heralded as examples of public-private partnerships' benefits to our nation's schools.

The Role of Philanthropy in Chartered School Growth

When chartered schools surged in popularity and threatened to break up the public education monopoly, the educational establishment began attacking the philanthropists who were supporting educational reform. Without a doubt, philanthropy has been a major factor in the growth of chartered schools. The educational reform movement is about twenty-five years old as of this writing. Within this short time, chartered schools have permanently transformed public education faster and more dramatically than any other reform movement. This has taken place, in large part, thanks to the financial backing of affluent individuals and their families.

Early in the chartered school movement, philanthropists recognized the potential of chartered schools. Many supported the development and growth of this fledgling model while also remaining benefactors of traditional public schools. When chartered schools opened their doors, community members quickly took notice of their revolutionary, publicly and privately funded education model. Parents saw the promise of chartered schools and enrolled their children in this new form of public school. Philanthropists were some of the first to identify the positive outcomes chartered schools were demonstrating, providing them with a tangible return on their benevolent investment.

Political Change

Nearly two decades after the first chartered school opened its doors for business, highly motivated philanthropists at the forefront of the educational reform movement saw an even greater opportunity to push chartered schools forward, beyond directly funding chartered schools and CMOs.

In order to bring about faster and bigger expansion, they would need to change the policies, practices, and procedures at the backbone of public school operations, a spine the educational establishment considered inviolable. Many of these policies, practices, and procedures were creating obstacles—bureaucratic shackles—that would always restrict chartered schools from fully realizing their potential. The state-mandated and local statutes, collective-bargaining contracts, and biased, elected officials were barriers. By challenging public school policies, practices, and procedures, philanthropists were challenging the educational establishment itself.

In an effort to remove the barriers that served as a glass ceiling holding down the reform movement's ability to fulfill its vision, philanthropists determined they needed a grassroots strategy in the tradition of other well-organized efforts to create widespread change. Similar to public and private entities before them, educational reformers planned to use legislation to implement new laws and policies—and modify existing ones. From their outset, local, state, and federal legislatures have created laws and policies that would benefit society. Changing existing laws and policies and discarding obsolete ones are typically the result of concerted efforts on the part of multiple stakeholders, organized by and for the people. Well-organized groups nationwide strategically stand behind the individuals running for political office in specific locations, lending their support to those who best match their legislative objectives. This legislative emphasis became the top priority of high-profile philanthropists backing the educational reform movement.

In order to effectively leverage the legislative process in favor of true change, philanthropists identified two areas of focus: First, charter advocacy groups at the local, state, and national levels had to be strengthened. Giving these groups the support they needed would allow them to influence the political process and provide a buffer between fledgling chartered school supporters and long-entrenched traditional public education support associations, such as those representing superintendents, school boards, and teachers' unions. Second, at every level of government, philanthropists would support candidates committed to developing a level playing field for those embracing a broader view of public education and its possibilities for innovation. When philanthropists shifted their resources toward promoting legislation, the educational establishment viewed this as a threat to its legitimacy. Suddenly, a formidable and well-funded movement was now challenging traditional public schools, which had not only previously run with unquestioned authority but also been the predominant recipients of philanthropic aid. Their monopoly was at risk of being dismantled by a market-driven approach. Outside forces beyond their control were scrutinizing their policies, practices, and procedures. Fear of the unknown is a universal theme, and the educational establishment used pushback as an effort to preserve its previously unquestioned identity.

The establishment has taken its case to both literal courtrooms and the court of public opinion. Those vigorously defending the establishment argue that, without philanthropists' backing, CMOs would have never reached their scale and prominence. They claim philanthropists are using their wealth to promote self-serving ideologies that conflict with the objective of public education: to uphold the educational social contract.

Throughout the country, the establishment is portraying philanthropists as rich individuals out to benefit themselves to the detriment of public education. But, as you have read throughout this book, in case after case, these same arguments can be levied against the educational establishment itself: It has put the self-serving agendas of its stakeholders above the needs of the students it is supposed to serve and has always welcomed philanthropic contributions.

At their onset, chartered schools were small, independently run entities that posed no present or foreseeable threat to the educational establishment. The establishment embraced and heralded the role of philanthropists in bolstering its cherished institutions. But when philanthropists began questioning the shortcomings of traditional public education and supporting the educational reform movement, the advocate was declared an adversary. With traditional public education and chartered schools' continued evolution, the role of philanthropy will change as well. One thing, however, is certain: Philanthropists are forcing the educational establishment out of its comfort zone.

Chapter 9

OBSERVATIONS ON POVERTY

Tom R. Davis has spent his entire career in public education:
first as classroom teacher, later in administration, and currently
as a consultant and executive coach to educational leaders.

CHILDREN LIVING IN poverty face greater challenges than their socioeconomically advantaged peers in their ability to learn in school. It affects their attention span in class, their ability to complete homework, their interactions with fellow students and staff—in general, their ability to absorb the material presented to them in class. In turn, chartered schools and traditional public schools alike are challenged to respond to this situation so all students have equal opportunity to benefit from their academic environment.

Like many Americans today, I grew up in an urban setting. Most of my nine brothers and sisters were out of the nest and involved in the workforce, college, or the military by age eighteen. This could not be further from the scarcity my past relatives faced; even though their roots were deep in the Midwest wheat bowl, they made the tough decision to migrate to the West Coast for work. Unsure of how long they would have resources or even mobility, my entire family relocated for fear of what many Americans still struggle with: poverty.

Unfortunately, for countless Americans today, simply relocating is not enough to keep them out of the mire of poverty. For most of us, our perspective on poverty is often largely influenced by our experience with it. If you have ever lived under impoverished circumstances, such as homelessness, your understanding of poverty is likely to be different from the understanding an observer of poverty might have.

In my case, I have only been an observer. I cannot recall ever missing a meal, not having a bed to sleep in, or not having clothes to wear. I cannot pretend to understand a life of poverty. Certainly, growing up, I knew people struggled with it. I knew my family gave to charities, as did I. But the signs of poverty were not visible in my neighborhood.

I recall driving to graduate school at Pepperdine University in downtown Los Angeles and observing people on the streets. I took the same route at the same time three days per week for two years. The neighborhoods could be described as rundown and in disrepair. Some people pushed shopping carts holding all their worldly possessions, while others sat on old furniture watching the day go by. I had been accustomed to the notion that most working-age adults spent their afternoons at a job or school, so in the case of these out-of-work adults, I wondered what their backgrounds were and what opportunities these adults had, if any.

My observations became an unscientific study of the snail's pace of progress in a poor community and the unchanging lack of opportunity that existed on the streets. I saw the same people in the same place at the same time, week after week with no job, no money, and no future. This commute brought me to terms with the face of poverty. I will never forget seeing the same five or six young men in front of a small neighborhood market, smoking and drinking from a paper bag in the middle of the day . . . every time I drove past it. They were not alone: People of all ages waited, wished, and despaired nearby. They did not have much available to them, other than an endless parade of cars to watch. And I, in the traffic, watched back.

The information I gleaned from this ongoing observation later informed my work as an educator. Certainly, I worked with hundreds of students born into poverty. The conclusion I drew was that we, as a society, *do* know that education relieves poverty; it is key in the fight to move communities forward both economically and socially.

Our society has this knowledge, and yet, why has our country not made greater, more lasting strides to eradicate poverty?

Solutions are often short-term and therefore unsustainable; programs designed to support growth and remove individuals from the ranks of the poor will last only as long as the funding does. A looming contributing factor is the lack of recognition and funding for the need to make quality education accessible for every American. Successful short-term programs never seem to become long-term programs. Therefore, education and those support systems designed by communities never endure long enough to make a difference.

During our research, we visited over a dozen major American cities. Poverty appeared in every one of them: St. Louis, Detroit, New York, Los Angeles, Memphis, Cleveland, Phoenix, Santa Fe, Chicago; the list goes on. We saw people living outdoors, rain or shine, snowstorm or heat wave. Poverty was disparagingly consistent.

Poverty was repeatedly a concern in schools, districts, cities, and states. Many citizens believe large-scale poverty holds us back from becoming a truly prosperous nation. Granted, so-called wars have been waged on poverty, and social programs have been designed to support those living at the poverty level. In the meantime, the gap between the haves and have-nots increases with successive generations.

Endless research has been compiled, and numerous programs have been signed into being, yet poverty remains a fixture of society. The fact that students have only a specific window of time to make the most of their school-age years makes the battle against poverty especially crucial. We have much left to explore when it comes to finding weapons that will finally defeat poverty for good.

Since humans shifted from hunting and gathering to agriculture, a segment of the population has always lived in poverty. At one time, to be in poverty meant no food, shelter, job, or clothes. Most people agree impoverished living conditions could and should be improved. Depending on the geographic location in question, a person or family can be identified as impoverished based on their income, size, housing, medical care, nutrition, and more. The complexity of data is so rampant and indistinguishable that the awfulness of poverty has been lost in rhetoric and multiple definitions. The bottom line is identifying poverty is not as complicated as some may contend. In the case of chartered schools, many have identified poverty in a community. They have taken timely, direct, and pragmatic action that has provided academic and social support. This includes health, wellness, nutrition, social awareness, and self-sufficiency for young people living in impoverished communities.

Much of the data relating to poverty seems to be developed and supported by a variety of special interests. Some data collected by interest groups show a downward trend in the number of people living in poverty, while other data show an uptick in the population living under poverty. Other groups seek to define policies and laws that govern issues or conditions relating to poverty. Regardless of the definition, level, or type of poverty, a child living in challenging conditions is less likely to obtain a satisfactory level of education necessary to become a productive adult than is a child living without those challenges.

What remains clear is poverty is a local and national concern. During our discussions, when we asked about poverty and its ramifications, answers generally fell under two categories. One group said, "We cannot improve children's education issues and learning until we reduce the level of poverty." The second group maintained, "We cannot wait until poverty is fixed to begin effective education of students."

Humanity and decency demand we care for our fellow citizens and provide for their well-being. Unfortunately, ineffective poverty-reducing programs have put a fiscal strain on local, state, and national budgets without any significant improvement to the lives of millions still living in poverty.

Poverty has less or nothing to do with choices and more to do with the socioeconomic conditions of one's environment. Without the resources and opportunities necessary to grow and thrive, a person will face multiple setbacks that will thwart any effort to reach a level of success as defined by any societal metric.

A review of the literature on the subject of poverty would lead the reader to believe a portion of the population will inevitably find its way to the poverty level. Some have found it reasonable to accept that 4–6 percent of the population will be identified as living in poverty, chronically unemployable, or homeless. Because the degree of poverty is also relative to the measure of a society's prosperity, the identified standard of poverty varies from region to region.

The causes of poverty for most are not clear but, instead, are complicated. Regardless of the uncertain sources of poverty, the question remains unchanged: What responsibility does society have to provide for a person or an entire family living in poverty? Apparently, not enough people believe we have a duty or responsibility to implement caring, long-term or short-term programs to eradicate poverty.

The cycle of poverty not only ensnares individuals; it also can trap families and communities. Men and women may have the desire to break out of poverty, but without the resources to do so, they have few chances to elevate their standard of living. For example, the massive industrial decrease in steel, shipping, manufacturing, and support services that reduced cities to shells of their formerly prosperous days threw people out of work and left buildings standing empty and decaying. Attempts at redirection, retraining, and relocation did not return people to prosperity. After the failure of these programs, poverty found a stronger foothold that has remained for decades.

Unfortunately, it appears a sense of urgency does not exist within government to solve the problem of poverty. Steps taken by government agencies have fallen miserably short. This fact reinforces the belief that poverty is a result of society's neglect. While people do control their own choices, the conditions placed on them by external forces will likely cause poverty to continue, unless education and educational options become a true priority for those responsible for creating policy.

How Does Public Education Connect to Poverty?

The thoughts presented above are an interesting academic and philosophical discussion but do not address the basic problem of how a teacher can help impoverished students learn. Research tells us a child who comes to school hungry (perhaps even malnourished) and lacking a night of restful sleep, which are common aspects of living under the stress of poverty, is less likely to perform well academically.

Teachers are limited in how they can address poverty inside or outside their classroom. The student has limited time to learn; each year is critical to the student's academic growth. While society deals with community poverty, the teacher must provide high-quality learning each day. Efforts to resolve issues of poverty must be addressed at the same time children are being moved forward in their learning. This clearly poses a great challenge to educators. So what exactly is wrong with public education?

What used to be a respected system is being singled out for attacks from many sides for its inability to combat this great societal issue: poverty. Is it too much to expect that a high-quality education should improve the quality of life for students, their families, and the community at large?

Today, a public education is extended to all students. Mass communication has helped inform people about the lack of equity within the many neighborhoods that make up a city. As noted before, communities have found their voice; they want to see change. The expectation is that, because public schools are the main vehicle for educating our nation's youth, schools must be able to deliver strong instruction. This instruction must reflect an assurance that the best education possible in one part of the community is accessible to all other communities. Those within public education know they are being held responsible for the delivery of results that will demonstrate their institution is the great equalizer. The classroom may not be responsible for removing poverty in a city; it is, however, responsible for creating opportunity.

Poverty affects educational outcomes. Business owners complain schools are not preparing young people for the workforce. Some students cannot even read, write, or complete basic mathematical computations. Political organizers, urban clergy, community-based organizations, and parents are frustrated about inequity, injustice, lack of access, and poor-quality education—and rightfully so.

Legislators are trying to pass laws that play up to well-funded special interest groups in hopes of currying a large volume of voter support. However, nothing actually seems to be reducing the level of poverty in most of the suffering communities. These communities are disproportionately represented by ethnic minorities. Career educators have consistently advocated for the need to improve the welfare of students while at school. Unfortunately, forces beyond the classroom are preventing a large-scale reversal of the downward spiral of poverty and low student performance.

While the simple cure to poverty is yet unknown, unless society provides reasonable, equitable economic opportunities and a basic level of education, there will be little to no progress made for these children. Thus, the poverty cycle will continue.

The traditional education system has been called out to reduce the poor performance of children in poverty in urban, suburban, and rural communities. Educators ask how they can be responsible for turning around a societal malady over which they have no control. It seems educators are underfunded, overworked, and underappreciated. Many feel they are shouldering blame for the poverty of their students, which they feel powerless to improve.

Research tells us relatively low poverty levels in a given population will have minimal impact on the socioeconomic development of a geographic location. Conversely, a significantly high poverty level will have dire consequences for the socioeconomic viability of a region and not only will negatively affect a community's stability but will also increase the potential for more poverty. The United States must fight to keep its poverty levels from rising to this level and above, and even though it is a challenge, educating underprivileged youth could be one of the only ways to prevent this scale of negative impact. The task becomes even more difficult, unfortunately, when faced with the influx of students who are not only impoverished but also homeless.

Federal law describes a homeless student as having no stable place to call home and living at an identified level of poverty. If a student is "doubled up," it means he or she is residing with another family or group of persons in a single house. This places students of poverty at greater risk of falling behind academically or of quitting school altogether.

To better understand poverty as it relates to homelessness and learning, we researched schools in and around St. Louis, Missouri, and other urban cities. The number of homeless students in the state has doubled over the past five years. Michele Shumpert, homeless coordinator, began addressing the problem with a change in terminology. She tossed out "homeless" and refers to these students as "in transition," which gives them hope for moving out of that situation. Her goal is to give in-transition kids the belief that they have something to work for, that there is light at the end of the tunnel. In St. Louis Public Schools in 2017, more than five thousand students have been identified as homeless.

Over one million students in America are without a permanent home. Their problems multiply as they grow from elementary school to high school. Lack of confidence, direction, basic needs, adult role models, and more all contribute to an uncertainty that drains students of time and energy, both of which are essential to learning.

The fact that US society has allowed poverty to reach such a point where so many children and young adults have lost sight of any path to the future is an alarm calling for immediate change. And data show the number of students living in poverty will continue to increase. The impact of recent local recessions unfortunately cannot be ignored.

Definitions and Data: Not Enough

Throughout our research, we saw public and private sector organizations attempting to curb poverty and its impact on schools and communities. Unfortunately, their efforts have not kept up with poverty's changing face. From the start of our investigation, poverty continuously appeared as a factor of importance but not the headline.

Every city we researched demonstrated some degree of poverty. Where we saw poverty, we saw hopelessness and depression. The reality is poverty is massive, continuing to increase, and those best equipped to address it seem to have directed their attention elsewhere.

Society has learned how to make some effective inroads, connections, and improvements: all short-term. These inroads might focus on temporary housing, meals, health services, employment, and relocation. While these efforts to decrease poverty have benefitted our nation's most vulnerable populations, it often seems as if poverty is so pervasive, widespread, and lasting that society does not know how to stop it or even reduce its growth.

We cannot justify society failing to direct more energy toward eradicating this condition, especially for the children so greatly affected by poverty. What greater way not only to improve the safety and happiness of millions of people but also to contribute to the overall economic prosperity of our country? Perhaps it is because, consciously or unconsciously, society has the belief that poverty has always existed and will continue to exist to some degree, as though poverty is a natural condition of humankind. We cannot support this concept.

Chartered Schools and Poverty: Replacing Inequality with Hope

When we began our research, we thought we would find a profile of characteristics that would make it easy for us to paint a national portrait of how America was responding to change. Instead, we learned very quickly that profiles for change vary according to regions. In general, the political setting and demographics of a region strongly influence how satisfied or dissatisfied the public is with its schools. These politics and demographics are critically important in terms of how charter laws are formed and develop over time.

In some states, students and their families were able to migrate in droves from the traditional to the newly formed learning communities found in chartered schools in hopes of escaping poverty. The new schools offered parents and students a viable promise of change and an end to harmful conditions in their neighborhoods.

Regardless of location, however, we were also deeply aware that the intersection of race and poverty desperately needed vocal agents of change. Even so, we were not entirely prepared for the visceral response we had when we witnessed ravaged neighborhoods across the nation. We cannot stress enough the need for change.

The decline of municipal infrastructures due to a shrinking tax base was shocking and painful to see in many cities. Traveling through blocks and blocks of what looked like burned-out and deserted war zones created a ghastly reminder of what happens when schools are closed. On occasion where a school remained open, we happened on what we considered benign neglect. By this we mean the tools for instruction were available, but there also seemed to be a lack of will in terms of a school's need to connect to students, their families, and the community. Whether this is motivated by race, we cannot say for certain, but we do know that benign neglect and its negative impact on all residents' access to quality education cannot be ignored.

We saw cities and towns teetering on a precipice of failure, going the way of those struggling urban communities we observed. The impact on our nation's educational profile has been devastating.

It would be wrong to ignore the plight of chartered school authorizers who are struggling to not only revisit their responsibilities in regard to providing policy and regulation that govern oversight of chartered schools but also create policy that best enables a chartered school to meet the needs of underprivileged children. If chartered schools have problematic

issues to deal with, so too do the structures within the educational establishment that are responsible for chartered schools.

Anti-chartered Pushback Will Not Stop Our Fight against Poverty

Volumes have been written about how education and poverty have a
deep connection to family, employment, quality of life, health, and more.
The consensus is that education is one of the keys to breaking the cycle
of poverty.

Even though chartered schools strive to elevate communities out of
poverty, they have been heavily criticized for supposedly making poverty
worse. Educational reform critics say chartered schools that focus on poor
communities only increase segregation. Unfortunately, even the NAACP
has spoken out against chartered schools in general. The educational
reform movement must take strides to show that chartered schools aim
to help, not harm, and are doing their best to actively adjust to the needs
of struggling populations around the country. Although some chartered
schools may have contributed to segregation, any such outcome is indi-
rect and by no means part of any widespread, intentional, and nefarious
tactic to promote it, which is the position maintained by the educational
reform movement's harshest critics.

Such an extreme position is narrow-minded. As Alan Greenblatt's
February 2018 article points out, "Unlike many public schools prior to
the Supreme Court's 1954 decision in Brown v. Board of Education, seg-
regated charters are not the result of deliberate public decision." Most
often, such seeming segregation is a result of location. Patrick Wolf, education professor at the University of Arkansas, says, "'Most charter schools
intentionally locate in inner-city neighborhoods that are highly minority
and are designed to appeal to racial minority parents.'"

Chartered schools are in affluent communities and socioeconomically distressed ones alike. They serve a wide range of communities. Furthermore, if chartered schools are guilty of segregation, traditional public

schools are complicit as well. If one believes that either or both types of public school reinforce segregation, one can find multiple instances to support this perspective. This accusation distracts from the greater, nationwide issues that countless chartered schools fight to counter daily in their classrooms. All of us seek solutions to societal strife and to end the cycle of poverty.

Those engaging in pushback attack chartered schools for worsening poverty when, in fact, the opposite is true. Chartered school leaders across the country have intentionally established schools where student need is most apparent and where the educational establishment has fallen appallingly short. For decades, traditional public schools have been the only free option for a community's children. Unfortunately, subpar student outcomes in urban areas leave parents desperate for better options.

An extraordinary amount of chartered school resources has been poured into some of America's poorest urban communities. These areas comprise families living under adverse socioeconomic conditions or large populations of ethnic minorities or both. And their success has been remarkable. According to the *Press-Enterprise*, California chartered schools with student populations comprising a majority of low-income students are accepted to the state's flagship university system, the University of California, at a rate twice as high (21 percent) as traditional public schools with a similar student population. Furthermore, "more than one-third of charter school students are finishing college preparatory classes in high school, compared to about one-fourth of their traditional public school peers."

Chartered schools have provided priceless hope for parents in such communities with failing traditional public schools.

Parents throughout urban centers have craved safe, welcoming, educationally stimulating schools for their children. Time and time again, chartered schools have come to the rescue and provided a market-driven education for families seeking better options for their sons and daughters. Chartered schools have applied the resources and cutting-edge, personalized educational techniques necessary to take students' eyes away from the hopelessness of poverty and turn them instead toward a world of possibility. The fight against poverty is far from won, but countless American parents can rest assured the battle is being fought in the right arena: putting student needs first and empowering parents with a market-driven model of public education.

Chapter 10

AUTHORIZERS

AS EDUCATIONAL REFORMERS who travel around the country extensively performing advocacy and researching public education, we are frequently asked to provide input regarding the most pressing issues chartered schools face. On one occasion, a county education consultant reached out to us for help. She asked us, "What's the best way for our office to guide the districts within our borders that authorize chartered schools?"

We have been asked variations of this question countless times before. Therefore, in this chapter, we will provide authorizers a road map to navigate the important role they play and the immense responsibility they have. We will outline how authorizers can fairly and effectively perform the duties they are charged with.

As Chartered Schools Grow, So Do Their Oversight Needs

Whether states vest their chartered school authorization to school districts, state commissions, county offices, universities, or other agencies, each entity is required to provide clear and reasonable regulations to the chartered schools they oversee. We will refer to any of these entities with the broad term "authorizer."

Unfortunately, our cross-country research has informed us that authorizers frequently fall short of their duties. As chartered school growth continues, authorizers have not invested substantial time identifying how to fulfill their obligations. In other words, most have not kept up with the increase of their responsibilities and caseloads.

The oversight landscape is rapidly and dramatically changing, and those responsible for chartered schools must take a new look at the impact the educational reform movement holds for them. They must figure out how to perform their jobs well despite mounting responsibilities.

Throughout most of the educational reform movement's history, authorizers were granted relative flexibility when it came to overseeing chartered schools. Regulations were open to wide interpretation, and authorizers played a low-profile role in a chartered school's operations. In fact, authorizers were largely unknown outside the educational reform movement and therefore received little public attention and scrutiny. In addition, authorizers oversaw charters on a campus-by-campus basis. Some chartered schools succeeded, and others failed, and these gains and losses were not viewed within the wider context of a national educational reform movement. Rather, they were evaluated on an individual basis.

But with the growth of chartered schools and the bigger role they began playing in public education, the pressure on authorizers to rigorously oversee the chartered schools under their watch increased. Chartered schools, once seen as an insignificant fringe movement, were siphoning students within a district's borders and undermining the long-standing and assumed monopoly districts had. The educational establishment's loss of market share caused alarm that turned into panic. It seemed as if it was being robbed of its entitled status. Consequently, authorizers became well-armed weapons of pushback powered by the educational establishment. These traditional practitioners were intent on upholding the status quo. Outrage over chartered schools even resulted in interdistrict conflicts. For example, in some instances, district B could approve a chartered school to open its doors in district A. Students within the boundaries of district A would enroll in the chartered school authorized by district B. District A had no control over the accountability of the chartered school so would put pressure on district B in hopes to regain authority over all public school students that resided within its boundaries.

Through our research, we discovered authorizer pushback started in urban areas. This is primarily because urban areas were the first to become saturated with chartered schools. Saturation brought to the surface issues districts were already facing, such as budget, staffing, and control. As new chartered schools continued to open their doors and districts realized they were losing students, a widespread disdain for chartered schools resulted. In addition, authorizers found themselves overseeing more chartered schools with the same level of district staff and budget they had used many years earlier. Supervising chartered schools turned from manageable to overwhelming and from low-key to burdensome.

Authorizers with well-organized offices comprising highly trained staff implementing strong policy were the best prepared to manage growing chartered school caseloads. Authorizers with a deep understanding of policy and an openness to work with chartered schools within their boundaries fostered a more collaborative and less adversarial authorizer–chartered school relationship. These well-prepared authorizers were ready to execute their duties. They valued chartered schools for the function they served and the role they played within public education.

Today, authorizers are charged to adjust to changing circumstances. They must review all previous policies and practices and ensure they are relevant to today's authorizer landscape. If a policy is obsolete, it must be discarded or revised. And when new policies and practices are necessary, they must develop them. In the following section, we will outline a process for authorizers to develop practices and policies that provide chartered schools the tools they need to continue to leverage their strengths, allow authorizers to perform their responsibilities efficiently, and most importantly, put student needs first.

Policy Resources

The first step to developing effective policy is to perform effective and exhaustive research. We recommend authorizers thoroughly understand their own state charter law. This is the fundamental starting point because authorizers need a deep understanding of what is required to implement a particular law. From this strong foundation of understanding a law's intent, authorizers have the information necessary to develop prudent local policy.

The second step is to perform thorough local policy research. This research should include focus groups that consider input from all stakeholders. In most cases, we recommend focus groups be led by facilitators trained to objectively direct discussions and keep them zeroed in on improvement.

Once a focus group has identified the advantages and disadvantages of local policy, authorizers are armed with information to move to the next step: improving current policies or introducing new ones.

Several state-level and national authorizer associations have published extensive guidelines for authorizers to develop policy. Many provide step-by-step instructions and clear templates. The National Alliance for Public Charter Schools offers quality information. While associations such as this offer solid guidance, we do not recommend any one-policy model be simply duplicated. There is no one-size-fits-all policy that will properly meet each authorizer's requirements. Developing good policy requires understanding and addressing each chartered school's specific needs, which vary from state to state and even city to city. Authorizers must consider the long-term implications of a particular policy and how it will be enforced and overseen.

When developing policy, authorizers should factor in chartered school governance. Chartered schools have made strides in increasing student outcomes in large part through their governance structures. Thus, authorizer polices should be rooted in state law and include guidance for profit and nonprofit structures, appointed or elective options for boards, conflict-of-interest requirements, open meeting regulations when applicable, and numerous other aspects needed for chartered schools to maintain independence while still upholding accountability and compliance standards.

Included in any policy development should be workforce guidelines. Historically, chartered schools have been granted a great deal of flexibility in their hiring and employment practices.

Authorizers must always keep in mind that local charter policy is not intended to replicate traditional public school policy. If chartered schools are forced to use traditional school district practices, they will not be able to develop new employment models. For instance, depending on the rules of the particular state, chartered school employees may or may not be part of a union. Thus, not all chartered schools are governed by the same workforce rules that traditional public schools must follow. Regardless of an authorizer's particular preference, chartered schools must be granted the flexibility initially intended in each state's original charter law.

Authorizers should also ensure chartered schools maintain their independence and flexibility when developing chartered school instruction, operations, and safety policy. Whether instruction is site-based, online, blended, flex, or any combination of the preceding, the type of school being authorized should be clearly articulated to the community at large. The school's leadership should be able to demonstrate that its leadership has the knowledge and background to create a successful school.

Policy statements for operations and safety should include guidance for building codes and permits, if they apply in whole or in part. Buildings must comply with the Americans with Disabilities Act. Authorizers should highlight the expectations for English-language learners, special-needs students, transportation, and health services. Chartered schools will use this information to identify the areas where they must demonstrate the ability to provide for the health and well-being of students enrolled in their schools. State law should clearly describe areas where chartered schools must maintain strict compliance, where they are granted flexibility, and where state law always supersedes local law.

When it comes to finances, authorizers should require transparency and accountability while preserving a chartered school's fiscal autonomy. Regardless of a chartered school's fiscal design, the end-of-the-fiscal-year outcome should always be revenue neutral, which means expenses do not exceed revenue. When designing local policy, authorizers should consider a chartered school's internal control, bidding and purchasing processes, responsibility for audit, and minimum reserve amounts.

Local policy also provides important guidance for use of facilities. The authorizer should know where a chartered school's facilities are located, its management terms, and who provides them. If chartered schools have access to district-owned facilities, they should have a straightforward means to determine how these properties can be obtained, the terms and agreements required, and who will be responsible for their maintenance, remodel, custodial services, and security.

The ground rules guiding the relationship between chartered schools and their authorizers must be very clear. This includes mitigating disagreements between chartered schools and authorizers through a logical process. A logical process comprises steps such as written notification requirements, meetings, mediation or arbitration, and possible legal resolution.

Realistic Projections

With shrinking student enrollments, the educational establishment views chartered schools as a threat, and authorizers are often at the front lines of pushback. While authorizers are charged to oversee chartered schools, the educational establishment has often used authorizer authority as a pushback weapon. The reality is, however, school districts often unfairly characterize chartered schools as responsible for the challenges districts face. When chartered schools are targeted in these instances, they become scapegoats. Rather than address the challenges or the need to adapt to change within their organizations, school districts often focus on pushback.

A superintendent and board of trustees are largely responsible for a school district's fiscal well-being. Chief financial officers, along with their financial divisions and administrators, are responsible to provide superintendents and boards of trustees critical operations data that is accurate, timely, and actionable. Therefore, accurate and clear data are essential for boards of trustees to design and then implement a sound strategic plan. Unfortunately, inaccurate and unclear data are a formula for poor decision-making, which results in poor outcomes.

Boards of trustees are charged with using public education resources to make long-term plans, including hiring, purchasing, and operations decisions, as well as projections for student enrollments and attendance (for one, three, five, and ten years), transportation, revenue, and expenses related to services.

Armed with proper planning tools, district leaders are prepared to make major decisions. Examples include whether to do any of the following:

- Rightsize their organizations to match services with enrollment

- Participate in pushback against chartered schools

- Work with chartered schools to improve outcomes for all students

- Identify why students are leaving the district's schools

A district's actions do not have to be reduced to one strategy. For example, school districts can rightsize their organizations by correcting an issue that has been previously identified in an effort to improve their financial positions. Along with rightsizing, districts can also determine how they need to improve and the costs associated with doing so.

Here is where a teamwork approach can dramatically benefit traditional public schools. Rather than maintain a categorical and sometimes irrational hostility toward chartered schools, traditional public schools can work with them to decrease expenses and increase revenue in order to invest in program improvement.

Well-Articulated Processes

Throughout the history of chartered school authorization, authorizers have been responsible for creating sound and practical chartered school policy. But the bottom line is that times have changed. Previous practices are not sufficient to meet the needs of today's chartered school landscape. Authorizers should now move away from their previous role and toward enforcing a clearly articulated oversight process. They should begin this transition by drafting or redrafting forms, documents, letters, and assurances that support implementing chartered school policy. Authorizer offices must balance their oversight objectives with their staffing and resources. After all, oversight and any subsequent action plans submitted to chartered schools are pointless if realistic parameters are not established and appropriate follow-up is not performed.

Authorizers should develop a schedule that indicates in what month certain tasks should occur. These tasks include authorizer and chartered school expectations. Furthermore, authorizers must then inform chartered schools when their visits will take place. Some authorizers will be able to complete visits within a few months. Those authorizers with large caseloads may have to perform visits all year long.

Authorizers should issue reports on their findings in a timely manner. Their reports must be well designed and clear so that from day one of a chartered school's approval, the school is aware of the study's findings. When authorizers make changes to report criteria, the process should always include the input of chartered schools. It is important to include the perspectives of those being affected by authorizers' decisions. While the authorizer board will always have the final say when it comes to approval, including chartered school stakeholders in the decision-making process reflects sound management practice and follows the model that has been pioneered in the world's most successful corporations. When all stakeholders are involved in decision-making, the process of implementing changes is made easier. Doing so ensures a more objective decision-making process that considers multiple perspectives and increases the likelihood that those charged with complying with changes will successfully implement them.

The process to effectively approve, renew, or revoke a chartered school's charter always begins with a well-designed timeline and support documents that are date- and time-stamped to verify receipt. Authorizers should send chartered school dates for public hearings or final votes or both. The format of the findings authorizers follow should be carefully crafted and used consistently. As public documents, they are subject to immediate availability to the applicants and public at large.

When a chartered school is at risk of having its charter revoked, authorizers must create documents specifically for this purpose. This is not only for legal reasons but also in the spirit of fairness—only when chartered schools clearly violate policies outlined in charter law should their revocation be considered. For example, financial losses to school districts and saturation are not legitimate grounds to revoke a charter. The most common acceptable reasons to revoke a charter are a school's weak instructional programs, fiscal insolvency, failure to comply with state and federal law, and circumstances where students are in imminent danger. Under these circumstances, authorizers should act immediately.

As far as costs for authorizers' services is concerned, authorizers should clearly outline costs or service fees that will be charged to the chartered school. Similar to revising report criteria, authorizers should work with chartered schools when making changes to fee schedules. If not, a dramatic cost increase may be impossible for the chartered school to meet. When developing fee schedules, authorizers should keep in mind that exorbitant fees are harmful to chartered schools and the students they serve. Unfortunately, some authorizers have used fees as a pushback tactic. This is one example of how pushback has become irrational, excessive, and unethical, and this strategy will inevitably backfire.

When the public catches wind of authorizer malfeasance, the response is typically fast and fierce. The public at large values our market-driven economy, and when public education embraces the free market, parents typically welcome the model. If an authorizer unfairly acts against a chartered school, public outcry will most likely follow. Thus, authorizers must consider the public relations consequences of any decision they make. Stakeholder communities are not mindless. They are aware when action taken is either just or unjust. Authorizers should avoid pushing back merely because a chartered school is operating outside the norms set by the educational establishment. They should perform their duties carefully and consider the broader public relations ramifications of any decisions they make. They are being closely watched, and if for no other reason, their actions should serve the public good now and into the future.

Authorizer oversight should always allow chartered schools the autonomy that is their strength. From the start, they were given more flexibility than their traditional public education counterparts to expand the vision of public education and improve it. Chartered schools were designed to introduce new models outside the status quo that work. They should continue to be encouraged to innovate and find breakthrough ways to approach how schools are managed.

Authorizers' Responsibilities

As you have learned in this chapter, authorizers are charged with immense responsibilities. The growth of chartered schools and pressure from the educational establishment to apply pushback will only increase oversight burdens on authorizers. Chartered schools can play a direct role in supporting authorizers and the work they do. This will not only benefit authorizers but also ensure they understand the challenges of chartered schools.

Through our cross-country investigation, we observed a clear trend: Chartered school leaders want to see quality schools that maintain the highest ethical standards and fulfill the needs of the students and parents within the communities they serve. When one chartered school fails to meet its commitment to provide the best education possible, this hurts the reputation of the entire educational reform movement, the students and families the school serves, and the authorizer who was charged with oversight.

A chartered school advisory group is one approach to bridge the gap between authorizers and the campuses they oversee. Collaboration begins with dialogue. This model has proven successful in many parts of the country. An advisory group would meet regularly to open up lines of communication, identify and resolve issues, and ensure chartered schools and authorizers always act in the best interests of the students they oversee. When every chartered school plays an active role in working with authorizers, all schools benefit—struggling schools receive the specific support they require, and thriving schools ensure their voices are heard and their needs are being met so they can continue to succeed.

Building a chartered school advisory group may seem like a waste of resources and time. But the opposite is true. Dealing with an adversarial relationship between authorizers and chartered schools is a resource-heavy endeavor. In many cases, conflict is both stressful and time-consuming. Worst of all, when energy and resources are allocated toward resolving conflict rather than improving the school, students suffer.

A chartered school advisory group would include chartered school leaders who would participate in reviewing newly proposed chartered schools, evaluating and providing input about new policy changes, and working to solve problems directly with authorizers.

When Authorizers Embrace Change, Students Win

When chartered schools succeed, students, parents, authorizers, and public education win. No doubt, authorizers play an important role in public education. They can enter a new era of public schools influenced by the vision of educational reformers and their challenge to the status quo. And they can adjust to change and collaborate with chartered schools.

Moving toward teamwork and away from confrontation will allow authorizers and the chartered schools they oversee to leverage their strengths. Both groups are represented by hardworking, caring, ethical, and creative professionals. When they team together, they can identify the most pressing issues public education faces and combine their expertise and effectively solve problems using their diverse perspectives.

Today, parents across the country are benefitting from a market-driven approach to public education. They have voted with their feet and demonstrated their steadfast support of chartered schools. Thus, any efforts on the part of the educational establishment to reject this model are futile.

While at times the conflicts between authorizers and chartered schools may seem huge and the ideological gap hopelessly large, instances of collaboration between authorizers and chartered schools demonstrate that teamwork is preferable, is possible, and puts the needs of students first. In the end, regardless of whether the model is traditional public education or chartered schools, when student outcomes improve, public education has fulfilled its role in society.

Chapter 11

CONCLUSION

THEODORE ROOSEVELT ONCE SAID:

It is not the critic who counts; not the man who points out how the strong man stumbles, or where the doer of deeds could have done them better. The credit belongs to the man who is actually in the arena, whose face is marred by dust and sweat and blood; who strives valiantly; who errs, who comes short again and again, because there is no effort without error and shortcoming; but who does actually strive to do the deeds; who knows great enthusiasms, the great devotions; who spends himself in a worthy cause; who at the best knows in the end the triumph of high achievement, and who at the worst, if he fails, at least fails while daring greatly, so that his place shall never be with those cold and timid souls who neither know victory nor defeat.

Shortly after our research began in 2012, we realized the momentum behind the chartered school movement had finally pushed modern education toward a day of reckoning. As we met with people from a broad range of sectors, we imagined a great oak tree spreading a vast system of roots. Chartered schools and their innovations began to stretch across the United States. Schools grew. Enrollments flourished. And it was inevitable that the canopy of this oak would eventually catch the attention of the towering, narrowly pruned, rigid tree of the traditional school system, now unable to view the horizon without a chartered school blocking its view. Whether it was in urban, suburban, or rural cities, we saw evidence of the educational establishment suddenly forced to take note that students, and notably fiscal resources, were being rapidly siphoned away.

At first, chartered schools drew little attention from the educational establishment. Then, an increase of students transferring to chartered schools began frustrating local school districts.

The battle to reclaim these students began, and although confusion reigned over how to address the loss of market share, local districts, county offices, and state departments of education turned to forces available to them. Unfortunately, the educational reform movement's unintended success has become a clash over who is going to get the students . . . and the funding.

The chartered school intelligentsia predicted there would be a leveling of sorts among education systems, but they never predicted a vicious bloodletting. Naively, chartered school leaders believed in a spirit of collaboration and hoped that the educational reform movement and the educational establishment would cocreate something better than what had previously existed. We believe, in the future, the clash between the two public education models will result in either a brutal survival of the fittest or a new, collaborative system that supports both educators and students.

We conferred with more than 120 individuals actively involved in the development of contemporary educational change. They validated how we, in our own minds, defined the actors in the chartered school movement as the good, the bad, and the ugly:

- The good were able to integrate sound educational practice with a keen sense of responsible operation and finance.

- The bad were perhaps well-meaning but were completely incapable of managing a school. Often, we found teachers who may have had some creative and innovative thoughts in terms of the school's instructional design but failed miserably in delivering an effective work environment.

- The ugly are solely profit driven. They have been a drag on the growth and improvement of the majority of chartered schools that are mission oriented and student centered. Too often, they may be missing the strong ethics and honest commitment required to realize a students-first public education approach.

Like some traditional public schools, problems in some chartered schools exist. Whether in traditional or chartered schools, lack of student learning and safety malfeasance have to be handled with a zero-tolerance approach. No doubt, traditional schools often have more resources available to them. Nevertheless, there is still a high level of apathy, unethical activity, and an overall failure to serve students within the establishment.

No movement is perfect, and without a doubt, we observed aspects of this educational reform movement that were inconsistent with our expectations. However, more often than not, we were gratified by the meaningful discussions we shared with men and women whom we can only characterize as heroes: individuals working every day with the highest levels of passion, commitment, integrity, honesty, and bold, tenacious courage.

The Educational Establishment Pushback Is Real

The tipping point brought with it economic challenges that have put explosive pressures on local districts to reclaim the students they lost to chartered schools. The educational establishment does not want to be uprooted; pushback is growing more hostile and aggressive by the day in cities throughout the country.

We have ample evidence to suggest that districts want to reclaim the students who have left their traditional classrooms. When California became the poster child for fast-growing chartered school expansion, for example, educators and politicians across the nation scrambled to slow or even stop chartered school growth in their states. Chartered schools in California consistently grew with a great deal of support and cooperation from local districts, educators, and the community at large. This growth was not unanimously greeted as a victory for students, however; soldiers of pushback sought to burn down the chartered tree by micromanaging chartered schools, denying charter applications, and using often unreasonable or even unethical means to prevent the chartered school movement from taking root.

The educational establishment is not above employing drastic means to shut down chartered schools. Pushback is not limited to any one action. It occurs during the authorization process, the accessing of facilities, the oversight of governance, and the renewal of charters. Across the board, pushback strives to restrict a chartered school's autonomy and freedom from local policy and procedure.

So how should a public education system react when it sees scores of students willing to be placed on long waiting lists in hopes of at some point being accepted into a chartered school?

We believe it is in the educational establishment's best long-term interests to work collaboratively with the educational reform movement. This approach puts student needs above self-serving agendas. The bottom line is chartered schools are here to stay. Despite an appalling lack of affirmation and appreciation from many within the educational establishment, chartered schools are clearly filling a void and serving the public good.

Throughout the country, parents are voting with their feet. Many desperately want more for their children and are dissatisfied with what the educational establishment has to offer. With the growth of chartered schools, parents have found a voice. The onset of a market-driven approach to public education has become a point of no return. Nothing will silence these parents that have seen the promise educational options have to offer.

Despite the support of satisfied parents and students, chartered school communities are challenged at every turn. In the end, we believe they will overcome adversity. The worthy and the willing will survive the fray. Those at the forefront of educational reform will continue their mission: to bring about the cutting-edge innovation that is their hallmark and, above all, put students' needs first.

NOTES

Chapter 1

2   **we spoke with Dr. Howard Rosing** Howard Rosing (executive director, Steans Center at DePaul University), interview by Mary Searcy Bixby and Tom R. Davis, December 4, 2013.

3   **report issued by the District of Columbia Public Schools** "DC Public Schools Release 2017 PARCC Scores, Showing Significant Gains across All Grade Levels and Student Groups," District of Columbia Public Schools, August 17, 2017, https://dcps.dc.gov/release/dc-public-schools-release-2017-parcc-scores-showing-significant-gains-across-all-grade.

3   **Normandy School District** "District Report Card" for year 2017 and district Normandy Schools Collaborative (096109), Missouri Department of Elementary and Secondary Education, https://mcds.dese.mo.gov/guidedinquiry/School%20Report%20Card/District%20Report%20Card.aspx?rp:SchoolYear=2017&rp:DistrictCode=096109.

3   **Clayton School District** "District Report Card" for year 2017
       and district Clayton, Missouri Department of Elementary and
       Secondary Education, https://mcds.dese.mo.gov/guidedinquiry/
       School%20Report%20Card/District%20Report%20Card.
       aspx?rp:SchoolYear=2017&rp:DistrictCode=096102.

3   **Detroit Public Schools** "Detroit Public Schools' Legacy
       Costs and Indebtedness," Memo 1138, Citizens Research
       Council of Michigan, January 2016, https://crcmich.org/
       detroit_schools_legacy_costs_indebtedness/.

3   **only 25 percent of high school graduates** Lauren Camera, "High
       School Seniors Aren't College-Ready," *U.S. News & World Report*, April
       27, 2016, https://www.usnews.com/news/articles/2016-04-27/
       high-school-seniors-arent-college-ready-naep-data-show.

3   **only 37 percent of high school graduates** Ibid.

7   **As Ted Kolderie explained** Ted Kolderie, *The Split Screen Strategy:
       Improvement + Innovation* (Edina, MN: Beaver's Pond Press, 2014), 21.

11   **examples of students enrolled in chartered schools** National
       Alliance for Public Charter Schools, *A Growing Movement: America's
       Largest Charter Public School Communities and Their Impact on
       Student Outcomes*, 11th Annual Ed., November 2016, http://www.
       publiccharters.org/sites/default/files/migrated/wp-content/
       uploads/2016/11/enrollment-share-web1128.pdf.

11   **Since 1992, 6,900 chartered schools** National Alliance for Public
       Charter Schools, *Estimated Charter Public School Enrollment, 2016–17*,
       n.d., http://www.publiccharters.org/sites/default/files/migrated/
       wp-content/uploads/2017/01/EER_Report_V5.pdf.

11   **In the ten years leading to the 2016–17 school year** Ibid.

12   **enrollments are approaching 20–25 percent** National Alliance for
       Public Charter Schools, *A Growing Movement: America's Largest Charter
       Public School Communities and Their Impact on Student Outcomes*.

12   **California had 1,248 operating chartered schools** "Fingertip Facts
       on Education in California," California Department of Education,
       last reviewed October 19, 2017, https://www.cde.ca.gov/ds/sd/cb/
       ceffingertipfacts.asp.

12   **in 2013, 19 percent**   "California's Charter Schools Are Putting African
      American Students on the Path to Success," California Charter Schools
      Association, July 25, 2017, http://www.ccsa.org/blog/2017/07/
      californias-charter-schools-are-putting-african-american-students-on-
      the-path-to-succes.html.

Chapter 2

19   **The giant falls** 1 Samuel 17:1–58.

19   **As Malcolm Gladwell describes** Malcolm Gladwell, *David and
      Goliath: Underdogs, Misfits, and the Art of Battling Giants* (New York:
      Little, Brown, 2013), 3–16.

33   **The most egregious examples** "Total pension costs for Fiscal 2018
      are projected to be $3.9 billion and total debt service is $2.6 billion for
      a total Fiscal 2018 budget of $30.8 billion." The Council of the City
      of New York, *Report to the Committee on Finance and the Committee
      on Education on the Fiscal 2018 Executive Budget for Department of
      Education*, May 16, 2017, http://council.nyc.gov/budget/wp-content/
      uploads/sites/54/2017/03/040-DOE-exec.pdf; "As of June 30, 2017,
      the Board of Education has $7.5 billion of outstanding long-term
      debt and $1.3 billion of outstanding short-term debt. FY18 includes
      appropriations of $594 million for alternate bonds, capital improvement
      tax bonds and PBC payment." "Fiscal Year 2018 Budget," Chicago Public
      Schools, last modified October 5, 2017, http://cps.edu/fy18budget/
      Pages/debtmanagement.aspx.

Chapter 3

37   **the *Titanic*** Wikipedia, s.v. "RMS Titanic," last
      edited April 3, 2018, https://en.wikipedia.org/wiki/
      RMS_Titanic#Rudder_andsteering_engines.

42   **In a 2014 Phi Delta Kappan (PDK)/Gallup poll** "The 46th
      Annual PDK/Gallup Poll of the Public's Attitudes toward the Public
      Schools," Kappan online, September 2014, http://www.pdkmembers.
      org/members_online/publications/GallupPoll/kpoll_pdfs/
      pdkpoll46_2014.pdf.

43   **chartered schools serve a large number of at-risk** "Similarly,
      27 percent of charter schools serve populations with at least 60
      percent of students categorized as at-risk." Ted Rebarber and
      Alison Consoletti Zgainer, eds., Survey of America's Charter
      Schools 2014, https://www.edreform.com/wp-content/
      uploads/2014/02/2014CharterSchoolSurveyFINAL.pdf.

48   **For English-language learner students, the vast majority**
      "Frequently Asked Questions," California Charter Schools Association,
      http://www.ccsa.org/understanding/faqs/.

48   **Even in cities where district data** Elizabeth A. Harris, "More Special-
      Needs Students Remain at Charter Schools, Report Finds," *New York
      Times,* January 29, 2015, https://www.nytimes.com/2015/01/30/
      nyregion/more-special-needs-students-remain-at-charter-schools-
      report-finds.html.

48   **But no solid evidence indicates** "Specifically, students with
      disabilities represented 8 to 12 percent of all students at 23 percent of
      charter schools compared to 34 percent of traditional public schools.
      However, when compared to traditional public schools, a higher
      percentage of charter schools enrolled more than 20 percent of students
      with disabilities." "Charter Schools: Additional Federal Attention
      Needed to Help Protect Access for Students with Disabilities," US
      Government Accountability Office, June 7, 2012, https://www.gao.gov/
      products/GAO-12-543.

48   **School for Entrepreneurship and Technology** "2016–17 Enrollment
      by Subgroup: School for Entrepreneurship and Technology School
      Report (37-68338-0122788)," California Department of Education,
      https://data1.cde.ca.gov/dataquest/dqcensus/EnrCharterSub.
      aspx?cds=37683380122788&agglevel=school&year=2016-17.

Chapter 4

66   **Detroit Public Schools (DPS) taught 156,000** Christine Armario,
      "As Charters Grow and Families Flee to Suburbs, Public Schools See
      Sharp Enrollment Drop," *Orange County Register,* May 30, 2016, https://
      www.ocregister.com/2016/05/30/as-charters-grow-and-families-flee-
      to-suburbs-public-schools-see-sharp-enrollment-drop/.

66   **we met with Robbyn Wahby** Robbyn Wahby (St. Louis, Missouri, deputy chief of staff of the Office of the Mayor), interview by Mary Searcy Bixby and Tom R. Davis, January 27, 2015.

66   **2013 census, the population** U. S. Department of Commerce, United States Census Bureau, "State & County QuickFacts, https://web. archive.org/web/20130912001257/http://quickfacts.census.gov/qfd/ states/29/29510.html.

66   **forty-five schools have been vacated** Elisa Crouch, "St. Louis Public Schools Tries to Shed Vacant Buildings," *St. Louis Post-Dispatch*, April 17, 2015, http://www.stltoday.com/news/local/education/st-louis-public-schools-tries-to-shed-vacant-buildings/article_4c24e3f6-9b63-51f1-8095-631579f5148d.html.

66   **white flight from the city** Campbell Gibson and Kay Jung, "Historical Census Statistics on Population Totals by Race, 1790 to 1990, and by Hispanic Origin, 1970 to 1990, for Large Cities and Other Urban Places in the United States," Working Paper No. 76, US Census Bureau (Population Division), 50, https://www.census.gov/population/www/ documentation/twps0076/twps0076.pdf.

66   **In 2013, Chicago Public Schools** Steven Yaccino and Motoko Rich, "Chicago Says It Will Close 54 Public Schools," *New York Times*, March 21, 2013, https://www.nytimes.com/2013/03/22/education/chicago-says-it-will-close-54-public-schools.html.

74   **Michelle Rhee, closed twenty-three** "D.C. Public Schools Closings: Chancellor Kaya Henderson Announces 20 Targeted for Closure," Huffpost, November 13, 2102, https://www.huffingtonpost. com/2012/11/13/dc-public-schools-chancel_n_2124915.html.

74   **Adrian Fenty, also faced political backlash** Max Fisher, "The Rise and Fall of DC Mayor Adrian Fenty," *Atlantic*, September 15, 2010, https://www.theatlantic.com/politics/archive/2010/09/ the-rise-and-fall-of-dc-mayor-adrian-fenty/344177/.

74   **Rhee resigned** Mary Bruce, "Controversial Education Reformer Michelle Rhee Resigns as D.C. Schools Chancellor," ABC News, October 13, 2010, http://abcnews.go.com/Politics/controversial-education-reformer-michelle-rhee-resigns-dc-chancellor/ story?id=11871446.

Chapter 5

78   **Center for Education Reform, strong charter law** "National Charter
      School Laws across the States Ranking & Scorecard," 17th ed., March
      2017, Center for Education Reform, https://www.edreform.com/
      issues/choice-charter-schools/laws-legislation/.

84   **Proposition 39** "Proposition 39 and Charter Schools," California
      Department of Education, last reviewed April 18, 2017, https://www.
      cde.ca.gov/sp/cs/as/proposition39.asp.

87   **In 2014 and 2015, more than one hundred chartered schools**
      Louisiana Department of Education, *Raising the Bar: Louisiana Type 2,
      4, and 5 Charter Schools 2014–2015 Annual Report,* December 2014,
      https://www.louisianabelieves.com/docs/default-source/school-
      choice/2014-2015-charter-annual-report.pdf?sfvrsn=3.

88   **In 2015, IHS parents** Sophia Hepburn, "Impact of Independence HS
      Sharing with 3 Charter Schools," iPetitions, https://www.ipetitions.
      com/petition/impact-of-independence-hs-sharing-with-3-charter.

89   **In Louisiana, as noted by the Center for Education
      Reform** "Anti-charter Assaults Fail in Louisiana," Center for
      Education Reform, https://www.edreform.com/2016/04/
      anti-charter-assaults-fail-in-louisiana/.

90   **According to the *Los Angeles Times* on April 11, 2016** Zahira Torres,
      "Charter School Awarded $7.1 Million in Case against LAUSD," *Los
      Angeles Times,* April 11, 2016, http://www.latimes.com/local/lanow/
      la-me-ln-charter-school-awarded-7-1-million-lausd-20160408-story.html.

91   **California Charter Schools Association (CCSA) published a study**
      California Charter Schools Association, *A Step Up: How Charter Schools
      Provide Higher Levels of California Public University Access,* April 2016,
      http://www.ccsa.org/CollegeReadiness_Web_Single_FNL.pdf.

92   **"states with multiple chartering authorities** Center for Education
      Reform, *The Importance of Multiple Authorizers in Charter School Laws,*
      December 2011, https://www.heartland.org/_template-assets/
      documents/publications/cerprimermultipleauthorizersdec2011.pdf.

95   **Rather than bring about rapid public education improvements**
      "Miles Durfee of California Charter Schools Association Advocates
      hailed the Orange County Education Board members' support for
      quality educational choices, highlighting that 'in an environment, where
      a school district board and superintendent [are] calling for an illegal
      moratorium on charter school options, the county board members
      have played a vital leadership role [by] … focusing on kids rather than
      adults.'" Gloria Romero, "Teachers Unions Trying to Take Back O.C.
      Board," *Orange County Register*, April 27, 2016, https://www.ocregister.
      com/2016/04/27/teachers-unions-trying-to-take-back-oc-board/.

96   **In Ted Kolderie's *The Split Screen Strategy*** Kolderie, *The Split Screen
      Strategy*, 21.

105   **In front of TV cameras** "The Education of Michelle Rhee" (transcript
      and video), *Frontline*, https://www.pbs.org/wgbh/frontline/film/
      education-of-michelle-rhee/transcript/.

106   **chartered schools are funded an average of 36 percent less** Rebarber
      and Zgainer, eds., *Survey of America's Charter Schools 2014*.

107   **most chartered schools are not compensated** Ibid.

Chapter 6

114   **New legislation, backed by the establishment** Barry Schmelzenbach,
      "Principal: Oklahoma Needs Discussion about Charter Schools,"
      Oklahoman, January 19, 2018, http://newsok.com/article/5580028/
      principal-oklahoma-needs-discussion-about-charter-schools. The article
      discusses the attempts to restrict chartered schools' ability to appeal to
      the state board for approval of new chartered schools.

115   **For example, in Illinois,** Lauren FitzPatrick, "Bill Would Ban New
      Charter Schools in Cash-Strapped Districts," *Chicago Sun-Times*,
      March 27, 2017, https://chicago.suntimes.com/chicago-politics/
      bill-would-ban-new-charter-schools-in-cash-strapped-districts/.

115   **forty-seventh annual poll co-published in 2015** PDK International,
      *The 47th Annual PDK/Gallup Poll of the Public's Attitudes toward the
      Public Schools*, September 2015, http://www.fsba.org/wp-content/
      uploads/2014/01/PDK-Gallup-Poll-2015.pdf.

116   *U.S. News & World Report's* **Best High Schools** "*U.S. News &
       World Report* Releases the 2016 Best High Schools Rankings,"
       U.S. News & World Report, April 19, 2016, https://www.
       usnews.com/info/blogs/press-room/articles/2016-04-19/
       us-news-releases-the-2016-best-high-schools-rankings.

116   **We spoke with Derrick Mitchell** Derrick Mitchell (principal of
       Normandy High School, St. Louis, Missouri), interview by Mary Searcy
       Bixby and Tom R. Davis, January 28, 2015.

124   *U.S. News & World Report's* **Best High Schools** "*U.S. News & World
       Report* Releases the 2016 Best High Schools Rankings."

Chapter 7

133   **Glenn is professor emeritus** "Charles L. Glenn," Boston University
       School of Education, https://www.bu.edu/sed/profile/chares-l-glenn/ .

133   **Harris is a clinical assistant professor** "Roger Harris," Boston
       University School of Education, https://www.bu.edu/sed/archive/
       roger-harris/ .

134   **both education experts provided insight** Charles L. Glenn (professor
       emeritus of educational leadership at Boston University's School of
       Education) and Roger Harris (clinical assistant professor at Boston
       University School of Education), interview by Mary Searcy Bixby and
       Tom R. Davis, May 16, 2013.

134   **"For the greater good** Glenn and Harris, interview, May 16, 2013.

157   **"Across the nation, charter schools continuously** "D.C. Charter
       Schools Take Bold Stand against Inequity," Center for Education
       Reform, July 30, 2014, https://www.edreform.com/2014/07/
       dc-charter-schools-take-bold-stand-against-inequity/.

158   **in Colorado, we met Nora Flood** Nora Flood (president of the
       Colorado League of Charter Schools), interview by Mary Searcy Bixby
       and Tom R. Davis, November 11, 2014.

158   **Colorado had 210 chartered schools** "Despite Funding Disparity,
       Colorado Charter Schools Thriving," Complete Colorado, August
       5, 2014, https://pagetwo.completecolorado.com/2014/08/05/
       despite-funding-disparity-colorado-charter-schools-thriving/.

Chapter 8

165   **In 2016, the Irvine Company, led by billionaire** Tomoya
      Shimura, "Irvine Schools Get Surprise $20 Million
      Gift for Arts, Music, Science," *Orange County Register*,
      September 27, 2016, https://www.ocregister.com/2016/09/27/
      irvine-schools-get-surprise-20-million-gift-for-arts-music-science/.

165   **"This gift from Irvine Co.** Ibid.

166   **Philanthropy is defined** *English Oxford Living Dictionaries*, s.v.
      "philanthropy," https://en.oxforddictionaries.com/definition/
      philanthropy.

Chapter 9

181   **Research tells us relatively low poverty levels** Gwendolyn C. Warren,
      "The Economic Impact of Poverty," Pinellas County Health and Human
      Services, May 17, 2012, https://www.americanprogress.org/issues/
      poverty/reports/2007/01/24/2450/the-economic-costs-of-poverty/.
      https://borgenproject.org/5-ways-poverty-hinders-economic-growth/.

182   **The number of homeless students in the state** Tim Lloyd, "Learning
      without a Home: How St. Louis Districts Are Responding," St. Louis
      Public Radio, May 9, 2013, http://news.stlpublicradio.org/post/
      learning-without-home-how-st-louis-districts-are-responding.

182   **"in transition,"** Ibid.

182   **more than five thousand students** "STL Public Schools
      Population of 'Homeless' Students Growing," CBS St. Louis,
      September 28, 2017, http://stlouis.cbslocal.com/2017/09/28/
      stl-public-schools-population-of-homeless-students-growing/.

182   **Over one million students in America** Tim Lloyd, "Learning
      without a Home: Students Can Struggle in the Turmoil," St. Louis
      Public Radio, May 10, 2013, http://news.stlpublicradio.org/post/
      learning-without-home-students-can-struggle-turmoil.

185   **Unfortunately, even the NAACP has spoken out** Valerie Strauss,
      "NAACP Sticks by Its Call for Charter School Moratorium, Says They
      Are 'Not a Substitute' for Traditional Public Schools," *Washington Post*,
      July 26, 2017, https://www.washingtonpost.com/news/answer-sheet/
      wp/2017/07/26/naacp-report-charter-schools-not-a-substitute-
      for-traditional-public-schools-and-many-need-reform/?utm_
      term=.91b07253f936.

185   **Although some chartered schools may have contributed to
      segregation** Alan Greenblatt, "Do Charter Schools Worsen
      Segregation?" *Governing*, February 2018, http://www.governing.com/
      topics/education/gov-charter-schools-segregation.html.

185   **Alan Greenblatt's February 2018 article** Ibid.

185   **Patrick Wolf, education professor** Ibid.

186   **According to the *Press-Enterprise*** Stephen Wall, "Education:
      Charter Schools Steer Students to Success, Report Finds," *Press-
      Enterprise*, April 26, 2016, https://www.pe.com/2016/04/26/
      education-charter-schools-steer-students-to-success-report-finds/.

Chapter 11

201   **THEODORE ROOSEVELT ONCE SAID** Theodore Roosevelt,
      "Citizenship in a Republic" (speech), the Sorbonne, Paris, France, April
      23, 1910, http://www.theodore-roosevelt.com/trsorbonnespeech.html.

ABOUT THE AUTHORS

MARY SEARCY BIXBY, M.ED, founder of eight California chartered schools, is widely recognized at the state, national, and international levels for her cutting-edge and bold educational reform leadership. She created the Altus Model for Organizational Leadership that focuses on improvement and high performance. A sought-after keynote speaker and advisor, Mary provides expertise in leadership training, educational reform, and the management of processes oriented toward organizational peak performance.

A former school principal and administrator, Mary fulfilled her mission of providing quality educational options to neighborhoods across Southern California by founding the Altus Schools in 1994. In 2015, the United States secretary of commerce presented one of eight schools

Mary founded, The Charter School of San Diego (CSSD), the Malcolm Baldrige National Quality Award. It is the only performance excellence award given by the United States Office of the President. CSSD was the first K–12 school in America to receive this honor.

Mary is a member of the El Dorado Charter School SELPA Governance/CEO Council and Vistage, a twenty-one-thousand-member business-advisory and executive-coaching organization that spans twenty countries. Mary has twice been a finalist for *San Diego Business Journal*'s "Women Who Mean Business" for her contributions to education and the community. She received the Harry S. Hertz Leadership Award, which recognizes role-model leaders. Her breakthrough contributions to education have earned her the Remarkable Leader in Education award from the University of San Diego School of Leadership and Education. The California Charter Schools Association honored Mary with both the Hart Vision Award and its Legacy Award, and she was a recipient of the Inspirational School Leader Award from the Charter School Development Center.

In her personal time, Mary enjoys family gatherings, gardening, reading, and writing.

TOM R. DAVIS, ED.D, is highly regarded for his leadership training, strategic planning, and organizational performance knowledge. For the past ten years, Tom has served as a consultant for Educational Testing Service, Total School Solutions, the San Bernardino County Office of Education, and The Charter School of San Diego. From 2005 to 2009, he acted as an executive coach to many of today's dynamic educational leaders. His unparalleled integrity, passion, and commitment to building sustainable, cutting-edge organizations have made him a respected educational leader.

After seventeen years of classroom and administrative roles within the Anaheim Union High School District, Tom was appointed as principal of Redlands High School. During his tenure, the school grew to sixty-five hundred students in grades 9–12 and became one of the nation's largest high schools. Moving to the district office, he played a leadership role in the planning and design of Redlands East Valley High School. He opened the school as principal and remained its leader until his retirement. For several years, Tom served on the executive committee of the California Interscholastic Federation, which governs high school interscholastic athletics. He represented Riverside and San Bernardino, the two largest counties in the United States.

Tom has fifteen years of experience as an adjunct professor at California State University–San Bernardino, University of Redlands, and National University. His courses included all subjects in teacher and administrative credential preparation. Under his leadership, Redlands High School earned three California Distinguished School Awards. In recognition of his contributions, Tom was awarded the Redlands Administrator of the Year. He has also served as Western Association of Schools and Colleges chairperson on thirty site visitations. He is a lifetime member of the Association of California School Administrators and Kiwanis International.

In addition to his professional activities, Tom enjoys family time, motor sports, water sports, and reading on educational policy.

INDEX

References to figures are given in *italic* type. References to tables are given in **bold** type. Notes are indicated by "n" following the page number.

MASTER LEADERSHIP TODAY
TO TACKLE TOMORROW'S UNKNOWNS

Our world is changing at breakneck speed. Only those organizations with leaders who skillfully and rapidly adjust to the seismic shifts taking place around the globe will survive and ultimately thrive.

Beyond helping businesses cope with today's challenges, we must also prepare our youth for the future. But without a map to guide us into the unknown, how will we develop leaders who can recognize trends now, identify changes on the horizon, and quickly adapt?

Fortunately, research into fields experiencing extraordinary change reveals remarkable leadership. As you'll learn in Mary Searcy Bixby and Tom R. Davis's forthcoming book, *Leadership Storm*, leadership can and must exist at every level of any successful endeavor. Both now and even more so in the future, influential leaders at C-level and beyond must demonstrate an exceptional ability to respond to change by teaching, inspiring, and engaging all members of an organization.

Based on interviews with successful leaders throughout the United States for their book, *Charter Storm*, the authors describe both what effective leadership is and how to achieve it. They address the rapidly changing challenges organizations face in the short term and far into a future that promises to be complex, volatile, and uncompromising. Your must-have guide, *Leadership Storm* shows how to successfully navigate an unchartered future.

Leadership must be inspired and taught.

LEADERSHIP STORM

By Mary Searcy Bixby and Tom R. Davis

LEADERSHIPSTORM.COM